Social and Economic Dimensions of Indian Population

Social and Economic Dimensions of Indian Population

Editor
Vatsala Srivastava
Former Head, Department of Economics
M.D.D.M. College, Muzaffarpur
&
Managing Editor
The Oriental Anthropologist

SERIALS PUBLICATIONS
New Delhi
In arrangement with
The Oriental Institute of Cultural and Social Research, Allahabad

First Published–2003

ISBN: 81-86771-19-0

Published by

Head Office : **SERIALS PUBLICATIONS**
4, B.S.S. Hall, Khyber Pass Market,
Civil Lines, Delhi–110054 (India)
Phone: 0091-11-23811659
Fax: 91-11-23812678
e-mail: serials@satyam.net.in

Branch Office : *4830/24, Prahlad Street, Ansari Road,*
Darya Ganj, New Delhi-110002 (India)
Phone: 23245225

Printed at : Tarun Offset Printers, Delhi

Acknowledgement

First of all, I extend give my thanks to the contributors of this volume for giving consent to include their articles in the book. My heart-felt thanks must go to Dr Vijoy S Sahay without whose initiative this book could not have seen the light of the day. I owe a precious lot to him. I extend my sincere acknowledgement to my dear daughter Iva for helping me in editing work in spite of being busy in her ISC examinations. My acknowledgement to the people would be incomplete if I do not thank my son Avijit for taking the trouble of typing and working on the computer. I am really indebted to him and bestow upon him my sincerest thanks. I extend my warmest regards to my loving parents, Dr K. N. Srivastava and Smt Shakuntala Srivastava, whose blessings have given me confidence to complete this job. I also thank Sri S.K. Jha, the publisher, Serials Publications, for his keenness to bring forth the book for the readers. Last but not the least, my gratitude to all engaged in the tedious job of printing, publishing and other related works.

Allahabad
February 6, 2003

Vatsala Srivastava

List of Contributors

K.N.K. Sarma, Deputy Director (Dev. Studies) Kirtads, Kozhikode.

Kailash B.L. Srivastava, Assistant Professor, Department of Humanities and Social Sciences Indian Institute of Technology, Kharagpur.

S. Firoji Alli, Faculty S.D.M. Institute of Management Development, Mysore.

Falendra K. Sudan, Post-graduate Department of Economics University of Jammu, Jammu & Kashmir, India.

P. Sivaprakasam, Reader in Cooperation, Gandhigram Rural Institute (Deemed University), Gandhigram.

R. Suriakala, Research Scholar, Gandhigram Rural Institute (Deemed University), Gandhigram.

Silvia M. De Mendonca-Noronha, Reader, Department of Economics, Goa University, Taliegao Plateau, Goa, India.

Ranjit Karmakar, Faculty Member of Sociological Research Unit, Indian Statistical Institute, Kolkata.

Bholanath Ghosh, Faculty Member of Sociological Research Unit, Indian Statistical Institute, Kolkata.

Sushila Jain, Associate Professor, Head of the Department of Sociology, University of Rajasthan, Jaipur.

A.K. Nauriyal, Reader in Economics, H.N.B. Garhwal University, Srinagar Garhwal, Uttaranchal.

M.C. Sati, Reader in Economics, H.N.B. Garhwal University, Srinagar Garhwal, Uttaranchal.

R.P. Juyal, Sr. Lecturer in Economics, N.A.S. College Meerut, Uttar Pradesh.

M. Mahadeva, Institute for Social and Economic Change Nagarabhavi, Bangalore.

M.L. Sharma, Department of Agricultural Economics, G.B. Pant University of Agriculture and Technology, Hill Campus Ranichauri, Tehri Garhwal.

Chandra Dev, Department of Agricultural Economics, G.B. Pant University of Agriculture and Technology, Hill Campus Ranichauri, Tehri Garhwal.

B.K. Khanduri, Department of Agricultural Economics, G.B. Pant University of Agriculture and Technology, Hill Campus Ranichauri, Tehri Garhwal.

Raj Kishor, Post Doctoral Fellow, Department of Agricultural Economics, G.B. Pant University of Agri and Teach. Pantnaga, Kanpur, India.

G.N. Singh, Professor, Department of Agricultural Economics and Statistics, C.S. Azad University of Agri. and Tech., Kanpur, India.

D.S. Singh, Associated Professor, Department of Agricultural Economics and Statistics, C.S. Azad University of Agri. and Tech., Kanpur India.

Introduction

India's population according to the census 2001 has well crossed the one billion mark having a decadal growth rate of 21.34% *during* 1991-2001. Providing good quality of life to the people by proper education, employment and income generation is the pre- requisite of the development process of the country. Pressing needs of growing population which is expected to add 200 *million* workforces by the year 2020 must be fulfilled by giving explicit education and lucrative employment opportunities. The coming generations, with the development of information technology and wide communication facilities are expected to be more and more aware of their needs and demands. If we do not fulfil their aspirations, a chaotic society might emerge with more cases of violence and crime, mainly arising due to wide disparities around. The main thrust of development lies, undoubtedly, on the shoulder of the government but to reap the benefits of governmental efforts the basic characteristics and mindset of the people must have to be changed. Nevertheless, the hard work of people and their collective effort can change the future shape and direction of the country's progress. Liberalization process started in India in early 90's which has, certainly, benefited the country. But in spite of the role and importance of the private enterprises, for the overall growth and development of the country, the government must be there and has to take drastic measures to fulfil the macro-economic formulations.

Policy of liberalization and privatization has made India an open economy and foreign collaboration, both in material and capital is reaching here in abundance. Being a vast country and having a population of a billion, India provides a big market to the world. Moreover, its human resources if capitalised well can make the country economically very strong in true respect.

Education and Population

India has to do a lot in the field of education. Literacy rate on the national level is 65.38%, female literacy rate being lower to mere 54.16%. As it is known, Kerala has the highest literacy rate of 90.92% and Bihar the lowest, even lower than Jammu & Kashmir. The other politically and socially disturbed states like Mizoram and Nagaland have too, in its comparison, a higher rate of literacy (88.49% and 67.11% respectively). No part of the country is said to have the population of cent percent literates. Female literacy in relation to male literacy is found poorer in Kerala too; at 87.86%, as male literacy is 94.2%. Literacy level, in all respects, shows the development of the society and attitude of the people towards educating their children. It shows that even in families where sons are given education, girls are deprived from its benefits. Population growth can be checked only by striking improvements in the field of education, health and socio-economic conditions of the people. A direct relationship can be established between education of people, particularly women, and the size of the family. However, female education is desirable not only for population control but also for improving the overall condition of the family and future prospect of their children and in bringing about various other social and economic changes in the society. Thus women can play a greater role in both population stabilization and quality improvement. Education should be the base for all types of developments-economic, physical, social, political, environmental, and ecological and various others.

Population and Sustainable Development

The first census of India, after the partition, in 1951 showed its population to 361.09 *million*. In just a half century period, India's population raised almost three fold. Between 1991 and 2001 alone 181 *million* more people have been added to this, as many as the population of Brazil, the fifth most populous country in the world. Sharp rise in population with a high degree of poverty and lesser degree of environmental and circumstantial understanding has naturally affected the eco-system of our surroundings. Over exploitation of scarce natural resources in a reckless and uncared manner has led to the degradation of the environment. To give the people a good quality of life means that we make maximum utilization of available resources, both men and material. But at the same time we have to balance between the arduous tasks of maintaining high level of development and making the depleting resources available for future generations. This difficult job is to be done for the well being of all, in present and in future too. Creating the environment of eco-logical balancing has drawn the urgent attention all over the world especially in the situation of rapid population growth in developing countries during the last century and the need for pacing the development rate faster. Till recently no serious thought had been given by the planners to this inter-relationship between the eco-system, rapid population growth, increasing use of technology and socio-economic development of the region. Researchers and social scientists today are busy evolving the way to get the development rate faster without unbalancing the present eco-system.

Human Resource Development

India's immense human resource can be utilized in the development of the country. It can be transformed well into the human capital. Since Seventh Five Year Plan, stress has been given on the human resource development. The Plan sought to facilitate development of the human potential in terms of self-respect, self-reliance and a life of dignity. In his foreword to the plan, the then Prime Minister Rajiv Gandhi had said "In the final analysis development is not just about factories, dams and roads. Development is basically about people. The goal is the people's material, cultural and spiritual fulfillment..... Policies and programs in education, health and welfare must also be restructured to provide a fuller life for our people"

Education and improved health facilities are the two leading factors, required for the upliftment of an individual, for his/her betterment and social and economic progress. To recognize this, in 1986 a new education policy was launched with the assertion that education should not be meant in the narrow sense of schooling and achieving a literacy level alone. A concept is involved in this which altogether necessitates for health, nutrition, wider employment opportunities, use of science and technology in day to day life and giving equality and special attention to the weaker section of the society. Education should become an instrument of people's development.

Gender Equity, Equality and Women Empowerment

In clear terms, there has been a remarkable change in the socio-economic condition of Indian women since 60's during which period rebellious voices protesting the male dominance in the society were first started rising. For centuries Indian women were put in the most deplorable condition and their rights and freedom were curtailed in a very systematic manner. They were kept in 'purdah' and were confined to the boundaries of home, deprived of education and knowledge. All these shattered their confidence making them unable to do anything in their life and taking a decision even about them.

After independence the Indian constitution adopted the principle of equality to every citizen of the country irrespective of caste, creed, colour, sex and religion. Women contribute half of the population and irony is that they are more unprivileged among even unprivileged sections. Gender equality means giving equal status to females in the society and in the family too and the literal meaning of the word equity in Hindi is *'samdrishti'* which is the perfect requirement for today's women. A number of legislations have been passed and put into practice; both on national and international platforms, giving the women equal status in the society but mere adoption of the legislative procedures cannot achieve the desired outcome in any field. We find that despite various laws in favour of women protecting them from social injustice and crime, ground reality is that women are not safe on roads, offices, public places and, in cases, even at their homes. There must be a change in the basic attitude of the people. They should accept the fact that women too, are made of flesh and blood and are full of emotions wanting self-respect and dignity. The world should be a safer place for them and they should be given wider space to live in and breathe.

There is found a gender bias in the society. Female foeticide in India has become a social evil today and its effects would be seen some time later when there is a large disbalance between the numbers of two sexes. According to the present census (2001) there are only 933 females in proportion to 1000 males. It means there are about 35.5 *million* less females in the country. Besides, in the age group of 0-6 years, 6 *million* less girl children as compared to male children have been found which is definitely related to some unusual and unnatural reasons.

Low literacy level among females even after six decades of independence, and technological advancement in the world, is another important phenomenon showing the poor status of women in the society. 45.72% women in India today are deprived of the basic education according to the data available. Education broadens one's outlook and a woman can better understand about her rights and positions in surrounding environment. According to the former Secretary General, United Nations, Boutras Boutras Ghali, "Without progress in the situation of women there can be no true social development. Human rights are not worthy of the name, if they exclude, the female, half of humanity. The struggle for women's equality is part of the struggle for a better world for all human beings and all societies". The policy of gender equality must have its effects on all sections of the society. Equality means equal opportunities, rights and responsibilities to men and women in all significant areas. This can not be achieved until there is equal accessibility for girls and boys of the education and development of their personal ambitions, interests and talents.

The first global attempt to provide better environment for women was made in 1946 when the Commission on Status of Women (CSW) was set up by the United Nations' Economic and Social Council. Its function was to monitor the situation of women and promotion of their rights in all societies around the world. The UN observed the year 1975 as International Women's year and held the first world conference on women in Mexico City. Three more UN conferences were organized in Copenhagen, Nairobi and Beijing in the year 1980, 1985 and 1995 respectively. In Nairobi Conference some 'forward looking strategies' were adopted, for the implementation of which the Commission was given the responsibility.

On the line of United Nations proposal, the government of India constituted the Committee on the Status of women in India (CSWI) to examine the Status of Women in the country. The comprehensive report submitted by the committee brought significant changes in the government policies regarding women's rights and status. The 6th Five Year Plan (1980-1985) was formulated according to the strategies set for women's employment and family planning. In 1974 the Research Centre for Women's Studies (RCWS) was set up at SNDT University in Mumbai.

A number of agencies, governmental and non-governmental, are now working to the cause for women's upliftment. The Department of Women and Child Development was set up in 1985 under Ministry of Human Resource Development for coordinating and guiding the efforts of these governmental and non-governmental organizations. Apart from formulating plans and policies, the Department's function is to implement the programmes which have been evolved as the welfare and support services for women, training for employment and income generation, awareness generation and gender sensitization. It has adopted a National Nutrition Policy considering the necessity of health care and nutrition for women and children.

The talk of equality and empowerment has no meaning unless there is economic independence for women. The view of Beatrice Were, Coordinator, NACWOLA, Kampala, Uganda, truly highlights the importance of economic independence in very straight and right manner, "you cannot talk empowering a woman without giving her a source of income". Economic independence gives a greater degree of power in the community and in the home too. Income enables a woman to have a say in key issues relating to herself and her development. Through economic independence women enjoy higher status in their family and get a greater solidarity and support. It also enhances their self-esteem. Efforts should be made that more women get the opportunity to enable themselves to earn independently.

The Department of Women and Child Development has taken up various projects to fulfil their requirements. The scheme Support for Training and Employment Programmes (STEP) was initiated for women's development in 1987. Its aim is to raise the incomes for rural women by updating their skills in the traditional sectors such as dairy development, animal husbandry, handlooms, fisheries and social forestry. The Norwegian Agency for International Development (NORAD) extends assistance for training and skill development and promotion of self reliance through income generation for women in non-traditional trades in the country. The concept of Women's Component Plan was mooted in the Ninth Plan document.

Other programmes such as Indira Mahila Yojana and Balika Samriddhi Yojana were started in 1995 and 1997 respectively. Rural women's Development and Empowerment Project (Swa-shakti Project) was launched in 1998 for strengthening the process of empowerment of women through the establishment of self-help groups. A national credit fund, Rashtriya Mahila Kosh, was formed in 1993 to extend credit facilities to poor and needy women in informal sectors to start their own independent ventures. Earlier, the National Commission for Women was established in 1992 which covers all issues relating to safeguarding women's rights and promotion of their empowerment. All these efforts have one objective and that is to make women economically self-sufficient and independent and to help them in attaining confidence in them. Assuring economic and financial independence for women is one of the most important factors towards improvement in their situation. The year 2001 was set as Women's Empowerment Year.

The National Policy of Education adopted in 1986 devised various strategies for women's emancipation and bringing equality between sexes through education. It was proposed to encourage educational institutions to take up such programmes which directly benefit and give empowerment to women. Women development programmes aimed to women's empowerment such as adult education, awareness building, female literacy, informational and training support etc have been started for the purpose.

Children are the greatest emotional liability for women, for the sake of whom they have to make sacrifices of their own advancement, progress and individuality. The women's work and advancement chances should be such that they, without disturbing this emotional bond, may be able to earn, either through a job or doing independent ventures of their choices. Employment opportunities for women will be said to be negative if they cannot find a job of their own choices, merits and educational backgrounds at their own places, keeping the pace between the family and career advancement.

As it has been said earlier, mere legislations and commissions cannot achieve the desired goal unless there is the required environment and no gender bias. Family as well as society has to change their attitude towards girls and women and take care of their emotional, economic, social and other needs in addition to governmental efforts.

To fulfill the need some specific actions are required to be taken seriously such as:

1. providing information to women of their rights
2. promotion of female education
3. encouraging them to form self-help groups for enhancing their income
4. curbing violence against women
5. taking nutritional and health care of women.

The above were some dimensions of the Indian population. Further, the book presents a picture of various facets of socio-economic changes taking place in the current day situation in the country. Essays in the book carry wide range of interesting topics from decentralisation of planning to human resource development programmes changing the basic development policies in the country. Some essays are related to the important aspects of women's socio-economic development putting forward rich material and empirical data showing their current status in the country, and suggesting ways for the further initiatives required to be taken for raising their overall situation. Arrangement of essays bears no definite criteria but the readers, in general would find some very interesting articles exploring new avenues for further researches.

The article "Decentralised Planning and Weaker Sections" by K.N.K. Sharma has given focus on the ideal experiment of decentralisation of planning adopted in the state of Kerala. The Five-year Plans are formulated by the central planning authorities for the overall development of the country and their aim is to reduce regional imbalances through planned development. For the purpose, priorities are fixed for the next five years. The time-bound planning involves assessment of needs and resources available for it and accordingly fixing of priorities. But in Kerala an experiment was made to mobilise the resources at the grass-root level through the direct participation of people of respective areas. This was to ensure the mass pressure from below for democratic reforms and to achieve the objectives. This decentralisation process has been named as "Peoples Planning Programme." The weaker sections of the society need specific attention to their cause and decentralisation of planning would bring a dramatic change in the whole process of development from the present bureaucratic set up to a participatory one. The author has very efficiently gone into the basic idea of the policy in his brief but well-balanced paper.

The next article "Human Resource Development and Organisational Performance" by Kailash B.L. Srivastava deals with the impact of strategic human resource practices on organizational performance. Today's advanced technical knowledge and economic and socio-cultural changes have made it mandatory for the concerned organizations/ institutions to have their own human resource strategies.

Only through this they can achieve competitive advantage. HR practices are related with transformational labour relations, quality of working conditions, incentives and compensation systems, training and recruitments etc. The authors in their paper have tried to investigate the relationship between organisational strategy, strategic human resource practice and organisational performance through the data collected from 20 IT industries and 18 manufacturing industries. By the detailed study, the authors have concluded that HR practices have positive effects on organisational level outcomes and different sets of HR practices are effective in different types of industries following different types of organisational strategies and varying financial turnovers.

In his valuable article "Population and Food security in South Asian Perspective" Falendra K. Sudan has discussed the pro-Malthusian, anti-Malthusian and neo-Malthusian approaches of population theory in full length. He has collected rich material from the eminent researchers' studies and put his analysis in the perspective of South Asian countries, namely India, Pakistan, Bangladesh, Nepal and Sri Lanka .The pro-Malthusian approach views the growing population in these countries as the main reason for the food scarcity and rise in prices despite remarkable progress being made in food-production technology. From the data presented it has been shown that from 1900 to 1945 the increase in overall agricultural output was overtaken by population but after mid-sixties growth in food production has been observed to be higher than population growth in India, Pakistan and Sri Lanka. In Bangladesh population growth has been significantly higher than food production. In spite of growth in agricultural production, the author observes, there has been general debilitation and lower physical energy and productivity among the bulk of South Asian population. Nutritious food is also beyond the reach of a large number of people in this region. The author opines that problems of poverty, hunger and malnutrition in these areas must be solved by first checking the rapid increase in population and then having equal distribution of wealth, income and other economic resources.

In their article "The Status of Women Work Force" P. Sivaprakasam and R. Suriakala have focused the light on the socio-economic condition of women particularly of the working women in the country. Women go for work due to various reasons; one being the trend developed in recent years of their desire to become economically self- sufficient. However, according to the statistics presented in the article their presence is very thin in the organized sector and being the least in the executive positions. The paper reveals that the number of women in the unorganised sector is many times more than that in the organized sector. Due to this reason they are denied equal rights and even the minimum statutory wages applicable under Minimum Wage Act 1948, Factories Act 1948, Contract Labour (Regulation and Abolition) Act, 1979 etc. The authors have suggested that for assuring equality, dignity, justice, prosperity and stability the condition of women has to be viewed in a wider perspective. There is a strong need to promote an entirely new set of attitudes and values concerning the role and status of women and utilize their capabilities in the economic development of the country as equal partners without any discrimination on the ground of sex

The next article is "Women and Employment" by Silvia Maria de Mendonca-Naronha. The study is based on the employment of women in the primary sector in Goa. The primary sector provides employment to a large percentage of the labour force in India and in this; women's proportion is even bigger. The main reason of getting accommodation of women in agriculture and allied activities is the general lack of skill which other professions require. The percentage of female marginal workers too in the primary sector is greater than that of males. According to the author the primary sector being an unorganised sector, the chances of exploitation of women by their employers increase and therefore the government should take extra precaution to protect the rights of such women and make legislations to safeguard the interest of these workers engaged in unorganised sector.

In their paper "Role of Women in the Self Help Group" the authors Ranjit Karmakar and Bholanath Ghosh have used the word 'cooperativisation' in a specified manner and have examined the possibility of cooperativisation at grass root level. The basic principle of cooperativisation is self-help through mutual help. Such Self-Help Groups (SHGs) formed in the Sankrail area of the Midnapur district, have been selected by the authors for study. These SHGs, though formed on the basic idea of cooperation, in principle they are not as such the cooperative societies. They have nothing to do either with production or consumption. These are the associations of women, not exceeding 20 in numbers, for the purpose to help themselves during the times of their odds. Along with the internal credit provision from their own savings these self-help groups have been linked with the banks, under certain conditions, for the external credits under the projects of rural development. From their study and analysis, authors have found that these self-help groups have enhanced the status of participant women as decision makers and made them beneficiaries in the democratic, economic and socio-cultural life. These groups, the authors anticipate, may enable the women to take active part in the socio-economic progress of the nation.

In her article 'Modernisation, Development and Gender Issues' Sushila Jain has picked up the issue of economic development along with social, cultural, psychological and moral dimensions of development. She is of the opinion that development must have a human base and then only it is development in real sense. The writer raises the point that development and modernization have disastrous aspects of environmental degradation but this should be kept under check. Development must be a sustainable one. According to the author, women have not received a fair deal in the development process. The plea has been given on treating women as partners in development rather than as mere beneficiaries of it by bringing them into the mainstream of eco-entrepreneurial and other development activities. The article stresses on the needs of gender equity rather than on gender equality, for equity is always about fairness and compensatory justice. At last, the author concludes that strategies have to be devised to change the culture of gender hierarchy which still has a considerable hold on the people.

The next article "Pattern of Seasonal Unemployment in Uttranchal Himalayas" by A.K. Nauriyal, M.C. Sati and R.P. Juyal is an empirical study done in Okinath block under the Okinath tehsil of the district Rudraprayag. The physiographic characteristic puts the block in a distinct category of agro-climatic resource zone. It has 7.9% of the total sown area of the state, and out of 2912 hectares of arable land only 68 hectares got the facility of irrigation during the period taken for study. Irrigation becomes difficult also with the increase in altitude. About 78 % farmers in the block are marginal ones i.e. holding land even below one hectare. The result finds that in a year as a whole, an average agriculture worker has to sit idle for 145 days, for some male workers the days of unemployment go as high as 175 days and females up to 147 days. The research can provide an ideal insight for employment planning where additional employment opportunities may be offered during slack seasons under employment guarantee schemes for marginal farmers and landless labourers. Such employment can also be provided to the workers engaged in other sectors like tourism and pilgrimage.

In the following article "Community Assets and Employment Generation under JRY in Karnataka",

M. Mahadeva has discussed the sorry state of the central government's employment generation and assets creation scheme JRY in Karnataka. The scheme was launched by the central government in 1999. Its aim was to create employment opportunities at regional level itself and so it was being implemented entirely at the village panchayats. Karnataka is one of the few states which have the highest number of villages per panchayat making the distribution of resources across the villages very thin. Inadequate public investment have by and large affected the asset creation process and brought down the public works. The paper has analysed in detail the pattern of investment under JRY and IJRY across different districts of the state for two consecutive years, 1999-2000 and 2000-2001. The author has asked for higher investment and alternative methods of funds allocation under JRY.

The article which comes next is by M.L. Sharma, Chandra Dev and B.K. Khanduri, entitled "Role of Women in Dairy Enterprises and Participation in Decision-Making Process-A Case Study of Smallholder Farms of Uttranchal". The district Tehri and block Champa were selected through purposive sampling considering the representative area of Uttranchal in the field of dairy enterprises. The relationship between contribution of male and female workers and yield of milk was established through simple regression analysis. The same analysis was made for participation of women in decision making and yield of the milk. According to the diverse data presented in the article and analysis made by the authors almost all the operations pertaining to milk production are performed by women but their participation in decision making process is the least. The analysis also shows that marketing of milk and milk products is entirely in the hands of male members of the family despite significant contribution of women in milk production in all the three selected regions.

The last article "Participation of Rural Women in Livestock Production System" by Raj Kishor, G.N. Singh and

D.S. Singh examines the activities of rural women taking part in the livestock production. Data was collected through multi-stage stratified random sampling procedure from Sitapur in Uttar Pradesh. Even though rural women belonging to all the categories of land holding participated in activities related to livestock production, women having marginal and small holdings had greater participation. Time spent by these women in their work was found to be affected by a number of factors such as age, education, type of family, size of holding, caste and socio-economic status. The authors have suggested that special training programmes should be organised by the government, universities, Krishi Vigyan Kendra, NGOs and other institutions for rural women to sustain livestock production in the country. This will improve income, employment and standard of living in rural areas bringing the overall prosperity

The articles included in the book focus on factors influencing socio-economic condition of the country and hence not only the students of Economics but also the people, in general belonging to other social science subjects, would find the essays very informative and interesting to read. As the world enters the third millennium, we witness economic and social progress taking place at an accelerated pace. The 21st century must be the century for India and not only the country's development should be fast but also it should be in every sphere. According to the founder chairman, INFOSYS N.R.Narayan Murthy, "A nation cannot build a modern economy on the foundation of a backward social and political worldview." The stress must be given on merit, dignity of labour, equal opportunity, freedom of enterprise, freedom of thought and action, secured family and moral values, democratic set up, tolerance for contradictory views and ideology and concern for the environment for the true development of the country. These are the basic building blocks of the society we want to have and must appreciate. Infant mortality, neo-natal and postnatal mortality, nutritional status, poor life expectancy etc. are certainly the health indicators of any society. Unhygienic living conditions, non-accessibility to proper and advanced medical facilities and even non-availability of timely medical help are some of the reasons for the high mortality rate in the country. To bring improvement in these situations the two evils, illiteracy and poverty, must be eradicated. For the country like India striving towards becoming a welfare economy human development has specific importance and for the purpose health and education become critical factors in reaching this goal.

Vatsala Srivastava

CONTENTS

1

Decentralised Planning and Weaker Sections:

The Kerala Experience

K.N.K. Sarma

Introduction

Planning is a technical process that involves assessment of needs and resources, fixing of priorities, preparation of projects and formulation of plans. But in the case of the decentralisation experiment in Kerala, the process of planning has been much more than a technical exercise. It was used as an instrument for social mobilisation in support of decentralisation. (T.M. Thomas Issac and Rechard W. Franke 2000). The mass mobilisation was intended to ensure that correct decisions were made at the local level, to bring about certain attitudal changes among participants and to build up mass pressure from below for democratic reforms. In the previous years community development was designed to promote better living for whole community with the active participation and, if possible, on the initiative of the community but if this initiative is not forth coming, but the same use of techniques for arousing and stimulating it in order to secure it active and enthusiastic response. Thus democratic decentralisation is a novel effort on devolution of power from top to bottom. The Kerala experiment on participatory approach to development which is called People's Planning Programme, now in its fifth year, aims basic attitudal changes towards development process among all the key players involved; the elected representatives, implementing officials, experts and the public even at the grass root level. The weaker sections of the society particularly scheduled communities have to achieve better development and its felt needs are so numerous and fast growing that the programs designed at all levels should prescribe certain priorities. Decentralised planning in the real sense would imply a dramatic change in the whole planning machinery from the prevailing bureaucratic set up to a participatory one. This would require a clearly designed Three-tier Panchayat system with District Panchayat, at district level, supplemented by similar arrangements at lower levels of planning at the Block and Grama panchayats. Proper devolution of power under decentralised planning becomes meaningful and effective when the people themselves become the planners at the village level as is being attempted in the kerala model of development started on an experimental basis from the beginning of Ninth five year Plan. This is in accordance with the 73rd and 74th constitutional amendments which prescribed a uniform Three-tier Panchayat system. Thus the bureaucratic departmental approach to development has given way to democratic decentralisation. The participatory motive of decentralised planning process envisaged the following basic roles to the Panchayat Raj institutions. (i) The primary role of the Three Tier Panchayat system is to encourage participative decision making at micro level by making the people involved in decision making process at all levels of administration. (ii) All the three panchayat institutions should strengthen the planning process by formulating plans on the basis of local needs and requirements as well as the potential development of the local area. (iii) Panchayat bodies should take care to mobilize maximum local resources and to implement schemes under different sectors, *viz,* physical infrastructure development, industrial sector and Social services.

Panchayat Raj institutions under people's plan campaign seems to offer an institutional innovation for planning from below. The on going decentralisation campaign in kerala also focuses on over all development of weaker sections by delegating responsibilities to the lower levels.

Weaker Sections: Their problems

The Scheduled castes and Scheduled tribes constitute the bulk of the weaker sections and their development has been the major concern to administrators and planners, while conceiving plans for these people under the Three-Panchayat system. The problem of SC/ST development in the state cannot be viewed uniformly or on the same scale as these weaker sections of society are not a homogenous group in terms of either ethnology or socio-economic composition.

As per the 1991 census, the population of Scheduled castes in Kerala is 28,86,522 which is 9.92 per cent of the total population of the state whereas the population of scheduled tribes being 3,30,967 which is only 1.1 per cent of the total population of the state. In Kerala, tribes are mainly spread over the following districts - Wayanad, Palakkad and Idukki districts. The scheduled caste population are spread all over the state mostly in rural areas. Recent studies reveal that while Kerala is much ahead of other states in the country in terms of quality of life indicators, the scheduled caste and tribes of the state are far behind the rest of the population in development indices. While the literacy rate of Kerala is 89.81 as per 1991 census, that of scheduled castes is 79.66 and that of scheduled tribes is 57.22. As per 1991 census 53.8 per cent of scheduled castes are agricultural labours. The work participation for scheduled castes and scheduled tribes is estimated as 41.2 and 46.0 respectively. The census figures show that 40 per cent of scheduled caste families and 48.47 per cent of scheduled tribes are living below poverty line. The living condition of scheduled castes is better in Kerala as it is estimated that 79.29 per cent of the total scheduled castes households own a house. Inadequate housing is still a problem in tribal area.

The specific needs and problems of schedules castes in Kerala appear to be (i) lack of sufficient land for housing and cultivation and (ii) lack of employment opportunities especially among educated unemployed youths. In the case of scheduled tribes, the basic needs include, land, proper housing, better health service facilities etc.

Past Experiments in Development Sector

In the past, it was for each development department to formulate and implement schemes for the weaker section in their respective areas. Decentralised planning in Kerala started in the early 1970's with the establishment of District Planning Offices and identification of schemes at district level. A major step in putting the concept of decentralised planning into practice was taken in the mid-1980's with decentralisation of the Special Component Plan (SCP) and Tribal Sub Plan (TSP). For district planning of the SCP and TSP, a Working Group was set up chaired by the District Collector and co-ordinated by the District Planning Officer. All the senior line department officers were included in the Working Group. Each department was to indicate the funds it set apart for the SCP form their departmental plan allocation in that particular district. The schemes were to be prepared by the Working Group taking the local conditions into consideration. For this purpose, a habitat and colony survey was carried out and a fairly comprehensive data base on the living conditions of the SC and ST Population was prepared. The Working Group was empowered to sanction schemes up to a fairly high limit without seeking permission from higher bodies. Every year, a plan was to be prepared and placed before the District Advisory Committee of Scheduled Castes for consideration and approval. The decentralisation of planning for SCP/TSP had a positive impact on the functioning of the schemes, but as there was very little popular participation, plan formulation remained highly departmentalized. Integration of projects was only formal. Besides, lack of transparency led to misuse of funds over time.

The Kerala Model : A New Approach

Decentralization is meaningless unless it is conceived as a total package of initiatives and policies of campaigns and programmes, that are meant to achieve total devolution of power to the lower levels of administration by democratizing the system for raising social and economic capacities of the deprived and exploited sections of the society. This is what is aimed by the planners in the state. While adopting a new approach in the development schemes which we call the 'Kerala model'. In contest to the previous plans and programs the Ninth Five Year Plan has been attempted as 'Peoples' Plan Programme in Kerala as a revolutionary step to address the issues confronting the weaker section of society particularly the scheduled communities. This exercise was to take district level planning on allotment and expenditure of SCP/TSP funds to local level with focus on local issues and problems. People's participation in planning under the Three-Tier panchayath system has the added advantage of raising the level of people's consciousness of their rights and responsibilities, which would tend to facilitate social change. It is quite obvious that under such a scheme of decentralised planning local issues would be identified and prioritized at grama sabhas. The active involvement of local public in the planning process would ensure correct identification, formulation, selection and location of schemes of local importance monitoring and evaluation of programmes. It aims the maximum participation of weaker sections in the development process. As per the directions of the Planning Board, 70 to 90 per cent of the SCP/TSP funds was alloted for productive and service sector and 10-30 per cent for infra structure development at the Panchayat level. The major portion of the allotments proposed for scheduled communities in service sector was on housing. While alloting SCP/TSP funds for infra-structure development it was insisted that 50 per cent of the beneficiaries of their projects should belong to scheduled communities. A district level committee consisting of elected SC/ST members of local bodies, senior officials and prominent social activists was formed to maintain the implementation of SCP/TSP schemes. Besides, expert committees would examine the technical aspect of feasibility of projects at each level and technical sanction to each project would be issued by expert committees.

In the meantime certain safeguards were instituted by the government guard against the misuse of funds by local bodies. Special Committees to were formed by discussing the problems of SC/ST households at grama sabhas and development seminars and a task force was formed at the grama sabha chaired by the SC/ST representative of the local body to oversee the preparation of SCP/TSP projects. The various expert committees at Block and District level is authorized to issue approval to the different development projects. Educated youth from scheduled communities are appointed in panchayats as SCP Coordinators to oversee SCP programs and tribal social activists to look after the issues concerning TSP fund utilisation at panchayat level.

Problems and Prospects

The distinctive feature of Peoples Plan Campaign is its focus on formulating projects based on the felt-in needs of the rural masses. A major criticism raised against the program was the proportionately larger weightage towards Special Component Plan/Tribe Sub Plan of the scheduled communities. But such fears were felt baseless as the decentralisation is actually reforming the already existing development process by democratic participatory process even at the grass root level.

The Campaign has yielded tangible benefits in the service and infrastructure sectives. Housing for scheduled communities has been given top priority in the Peoples Plan. During the first three years of the Ninth Plan, a total of 1,64,998 houses have been constructed for SC/ST families through the local bodies, Scheduled Caste/Scheduled Tribe development Departments and the Rural Development Department. The evaluation studies conducted by Kerala Institute for Research Training and Development Studies of Scheduled Castes and Scheduled Tribes (KIRTADS) in few selected districts reveal that a few houses constructed under the scheme are either half-constructed or half repaired due to the insufficient allocation of funds under this head. Sanitation and hygiene was another priority of the local bodies and it appears that in the first three years of the plan period majority of the house holds were provided latrines.

Due to decentralisation, the major portion of the funds allotted under Power and Water supply scheme are not vested with local bodies. Even after three years of implementation of the plan, this issue is yet to be solved. Such schemes are launched in tribal settlements without conducting careful feasibility studies. There is acute problem of drinking water despite huge funds were spent for implementing water supply schemes in tribal areas. Although electrificication of SC/ST houses was given due consideration by local bodies under Peoples Plan, a number of houses are found without the facility of electricity.

Despite the controversies that broke out regarding the genuineness of beneficiary committees engaged in implementing road construction works in SC/ST Colonies, There has not been much criticism on the effectiveness in implementation.

Consequent on devolution of power to the bottom, personnel from various development departments have been provided in all District, Block and Grama panchayats for the formulation and implementation of SCP/TSP programmes. The services of these officials help the various panchayat bodies in the planning, implementing and monitoring of SC/ ST development schemes.

Despite opportunities have been created for scheduled communities to actively participates in the different phases of plan formulation and implementation under Peoples Plan Compaign "an unfortunate fact underlying the programmes meant for the weaker sections have been the assumption that their problem is administrative in character." (Kunhaman. M. 1990).

Devolution of Power : How Far Achieved

Decentralised planning under the Three-Tier Panchayat system is expected to achieve better peoples' participation because the local people have a better perception of their needs and better information about local resources. This participatory approach in planning has the added advantage of raising the level of people's consciousness especially that of the weaker sections of society- of their rights and responsibilities which in turn would facilitate social change. The active involvement of all sections of people would be useful in the proper identification, formulation, selection and location of schemes attuned to the felt needs of the people.

The Kerala experience of development through Peoples Plan Program has made an attempt to create opportunities for ordinary citizens to actively participate in the different phases of plan formulation and implementation. Recent evaluation studies conducted in various parts of the state reveal that genuine participation in the sense that involvement of all section of people in the society in the implementation and monitoring of the schemes could not be seen particularly among weaker sections. Such an improvement can take place only when these much deprived population would be made conscious about the limitations and continuously strive to overcome them. The grama sabhas which provided an ideal forum for people in every locality to meet and discuss problems could not bring about effective participation of ordinary people particularly from the SC/ST households.

Another major objective envisaged under the Peoples' Compaign has been to improve the local bodies to prepare and implement their own development plans. The Kerala experience on such devolution of power has succeeded to a great extent in achieving this objective. The following assessment made by the Committee on decentralisation of powers (1999) is worthnoting in this context:

"The Peoples Planning Campaign, which represents the development facet of decentralisation, has succeeded in a large measure in deepening the process of decentralisation, bringing about qualitative changes in planning and implementation and alerting the mindset about participatory development."

Conclusion

To sum up, it can be said that the various efforts made by Keral State under Peoples Plan Comaign for the devolution of power to the grass root level have created a new enthusiasm among the common people including weaker sections. Decentralised planning being carried out in the state still has a very long way to go before its true ends can be realised. At the same time this new experiment has made an average citizen more conscious of his rights than before.

REFERENCES

Thomas Isaac. T.M., Richard W. Franke (2000) 'Local democracy and development, Peoples Campaign for Decentralised planning in Kerala, Left world books, New Delhi.

Kunhaman. M. (1990) 'Economic Development and Social Change' Research Review Publication Committee, University of Kerala, Trivandrum.

S.N. Mishra, Lokesh Kumar, Chaitali Pal (1996) 'New Panchayath Raj in Action'; Mittal Publications, New Delhi.

Report submitted on review meeting of National Commission for SC/ST, (2000) SC/ST Development Department, Govt. of Kerala, Thruvanathapuram.

Committee on Decentralisation of Powers (1999): Final Report: Strengthening of Professional and Ministrial Support to Local Government, Government of Kerala, Thriruvanathapuram.

2

Human Resource Development and Organisational Performance: A Strategic Perspective

Kailash B.L. Srivastava & S. Firoj Alli

Introduction

The impact of strategic human resource practices on organisational performance has emerged as a dominant research agenda as people issues have come to the forefront in the new paradigm of business. Technical, economic and social-cultural changes are leading organisations to depend more and more on human resources to achieve their objectives. Business results can be achieved only when human resource policies, pactices and procedures are satisfying the needs of the organisation, and that is why a strategic perspective human resource development is requied. Its development reflects the interdependencies of strategy and human resource mamagement practices. HR Strategies have been aligned with corporate strategy to achieve competitive advantage. Various models have been proposed in the literature to explain the relationship of human resource development with stragegy such as Schuler's model of HR strategy (1992). Another model by Bamberger and Phillips (1991) tried to explain the role of environmental variables, which mediate the relationship of HR strategy with business strategy. Walker (1992) has proposed a model, where he tried to align the mamagement of human resource with strategy. Legnick-Hall and Legnick-Hall (1988) tried to show the interdependence between business strategy and human resource strategy.

The relationship of various HR activities was found to be positively related with organisational level outcomes such as stock performance, productivity, profit, quality, and organisational growth and development. Many studies have quantified the impact of HR practices on firm's financial performance. Financial turnover and productivity was related with job security, union presence, compensation, culture, and demographics (Huselid, 1995). Leonard (1990) showed that organisations having long-term incentive plan had better return on equity compared to those organisations that did not have them.

Productivity has been linked with certain HR practices such as transformational labour relations, quality of working life programmes, quality circles, practices in training and recruiting, incentive, and compensation systems (Gershenfeld, 1991; Katz, Kochan, & Keefe, 1987; Weitzman & Kruse, 1990). Russel, Terborg, and Powers (1985) found a positive relationship between organisational level support and training with job performance. Tepsta and Rozell 1993 studied the relationship of staffing practices with organisational level measures of performance and identified five 'best' staffing practices having a moderate positive relationship with orgnisational performance. Appraisal system of the organisation has been linked with job behaviour as well as orgnaisational performance (Boreman, 1991). Many studies have focused on HR pracdtices and financial performance in specific industries. HR practices such as innovative work practices, which include incentive pay, teams, flexible job assignments, employment security, and training help to achieve higher lvels of productivity (Ichniowski, Shaw, & Prennushi, 1993; Arthur, 1994). MacDuffie (1995) found a positive relationship between a bundle of integrated HR practices and productivity and quality in automotive plants. These studies demonstrate a positive relationship between HR practices and firm results, more specifically of individual HR practices or in individual industries.

Society of Human Resouce Management conducted another major study (Ostroff, 1995) and correlated the quality of HR to four financial measures namely, market/book value (based on stock price divided by those assets representing 'value added' by management), productivity (monetary value of sales divided by number of employees), market value (stock price multiplied by outstanding shares) and sales. Analysis of data showed that all four financial measures increased dramatically with the quality of HR practices. Arthur (1994) identified two types of HR systems-control systems and commitment systems. He found that a specific combination of HR policies and practices are useful in predicting performance and turnover. Commitment type of HR system, which is characterised by high employee involvement in decision making participation in programmes, training in group problem sloving, and socialisation is related to higher productivity and lower employee turnover. Lam & White (1998) examined the strategic role of HR in corporate performance and found that companies with the strong HR orientation performed better than firms with a lesser degree of HR orientation. Guthree and Dutta (1998) explored the relationship among corporate strategy, executive selection and firm performance and found a positive relationship between selection practices and firm performance. Gratton, Hailey, Stiles, and Truss (1999) tried to understand and model how business strategies are translated through HR strategies and people processes into individual and organisational performance, and provided a map for translation and discussed about some people processes related to business strategy.

Harel and Tzafrir (1999) found that HRM practices had significant impact on both the perceived organisational and market performance of the organisation in public and private sector in Israel. They found that training practices are related with organisational performance, and selection and training practices affect the perceived market performance. Becker and Huselid (1999) in study of five leading firms found that a value added HR function is a business strategy that relis on people as a source of competitive advantage, and a management culture that embraces that belief. It is characterised by operational excellence, a focus on client service for individual employees, and delivery at lowest possible cost. It requires HR Managers to understand the human capital implication of business problems and can access or modify the HR systems to solve these problems.

Sheppeck and Miletello (2000) found that we could achieve better organisational performance by adopting strategic configuration of HR pactices. Fey and Pavlovskaya (2000) studied 101 foreign firm to examine the effect of HRM practices on firm's performance in Russia and found that HR outcomes such as motivation retention and development were mediating variables between HRM practices and firm performance. Non-technical training and high salary has their effect on HR outcomes for non-managerial people. There was a positive relationship between merit based promotion and firm performance.

These studies demonstrate a positive relationship between HR practices and firm's financial results. It also means that organisational strategy should be aligned with HR practices to achieve better performance. Organisations should adopt and implement those HR practices, which are consistent with organisation strategy. Organisational performance is treated as a dependent measure. Other dependent measures include productivity, profits, customer satisfaction, and shareholder's return. These measures will vary with the level of analysis, if at the corporate level capital market measures are taken. At the middle management level the focus is on profit, market share, and growth. If firms are taken as the unit of analysis, then we have to explore the relationship of HR practices, corporate strategy, and performance with each other. However, firms may also differ with rspect to size, technology, and type of industry. HR practices within the firm may also vary. Thus, in case of a single industry group or company, we can take dependent measures such as growth, market share, and profit at the business level. In case of diverse business units, we have to adopt some standard measures such as market share, profitability or growth. It may also happen that one set of HR practices are related to profitability and growth but not related to market share, while another set of HR practices produce a totally different types of results. The major question still not answered, is why this relationship exists and how it operates. If we follow the steps linking these two functions, we can probably explore the nature of relationship and the process involved.

Design of the Study

The present study followed an exploratory framework to investigage the relationship between organisational strategy, strategic human resource practices, and organisational performance. Organisational strategy considered to an important factor was classified into four types-prospectors, defenders, analysers, and reactors, based on Miles and Snow's (1978) conceptualisation. It was found to be a predictor of organisational performance, and this also had implications for HR policies. Innovation was used to identify organisational strategy, and organisations were classified into prospectors, defenders, and analysers based on the level of their innovation.

Strategic HR literature has proposed three differnt perspectives to explain the relationship between HR practices and organisational strategy, namely universalistic, contingency and configurational perspective. The universalistic perspective argues in favour of best strategic HR practices which is universally effective in all organisations. The contingency perspective states that the effectiveness of HR practices is contingent upon organisational strategy. Configurational strategy argues for a best fit or configuration between HR practices and organisational strategy (Delery & Doty, 1996). It was examined that which perspective is appropriate for Indian organisations making them more effective. People oriented HR practices helps in developing a positive HR climate, which facilitate to improve the performance of the organisation. HR climate was also measured to find out the prevailing OCTPAC culture in organisations. Organisational performance was measured using some objective criteria like profit, growth (in terms of market shae), and employee turnover. The major objectives of this study were as follows—

1. To study of impact of the type of industry and organisational strategy on HR practices.
2. To find out the effective HR practices for better organisational performance and in different types of organisations.
3. To investigate those HR practices that best fits under differnt organisational strategy in different type of organisations.
4. To study the influence of the size of the organisation (in terms of financial turnover) on HR practices.
5. To study the influence of HRD climate on organisational performance.

METHOD

Sample

The data were collected from 20 information technology industries and 18 manufacturing industries through structured interview schedule. Data were collected from top management regarding the organisational strategy from each organisation. Data regarding the HR practices were collected from HR managers, and other functionaries, and the HR department provided the data on HR climate prevailing in the industry.

Measures

In this study a number of dimensions related to HR practices were explored such as internal career opportunities, training, result oriented appraisal, employment security, participation, job description, and profit sharing. From the strategic HR perspective, some other dimensions were included such as HRD philosophy of the organisation and its liaison with top management, directing HR efforts to goals and objective of the organisations, human process research, creating business linkages and synergies with other systems, and networking. HRD climate survey (Rao, 2000) was conducted to find out the various facilitating factors responsible for the implementation of HR systems and procedures such as openness, confrontation, trust, autonomy, proaction, authenticity, and collaboration.

In the present study, strategic HRM perspectives, HR practices, and HR climate were treated as independent variables. Market share (per cent of growth), profit, return on assets (calculated by dividing net profit after tax by total assets), and percentage of employee turnover were treated as dependent measures for organisational level outcomes. Organisational strategy and financial turnover were the control variables. The study was carried out in information technology industries and manufacturing organisations to bring about the significance of different HR practices, strategic HR dimensions, HR climate in these organisations and how these variables are related with better organisational performance such as profit, growth, and employee turnover.

RESULTS AND DISCUSSION

To recapitulate the major objective of this study was to examine the relationship between organisational strategy, human resource practices, strategic human resource perspectives, HR climate, and organisational performance. Data from 38 organisations were analysed with the help of statistical software (SPSS). The results of the study are being discussed below.

Organisational strategy followed by organisations was identified. It was found that out of 38 organisations 10 were prospectors, 16 as defenders, and 12 were analysers. Among these one IT industry and 9 manufacturing industries were prospectors. Again 9 IT and 7 manufacturing industries were defenders, and 8 IT and 4 manufacturing industries were analysers. These results suggest that only few companaies were following innovative stragegies for their growth and development, while some of them were trying to select strategies only after carefully analysing the situation. Many of these organisations were defensive in their approach and reacting to the needs and demands of the market in order to survive and remain productive. Thus only few companies were competing and had experienced growth using an innovative strategy.

Organisational strategy necessitates certain behavioural requirements for success. Strategic HR practices can help organisations in this direction so that employees make the desired behaviour for better performance. Thus organisations should follow such strategic HR practices, which ensure that individuals with the required abilities put in their best effort, and are motivated to perform better. It would result in an increase in profit, market share, and low employee turnover.

Effective HR practices such as internal career opportunities, training, result oriented appraisal, job security, participation, job description, and profit sharing was measured. It was found that out of 38 organisations, 29 organisations (13 IT and 16 manufacturing) were effectively following these practices by putting more emphasis on the growth and development of the employees. Rest 9 organisations were not effective along these dimensions and they were not treating human resources as an asset, and did not follow those HR practices, which were satisfying the needs and requirements of the people.

Table 1: Effective HR Practices

Type of Industries	*Number of Effective Organisations*	*Number of not Effective Organisations*
Information Technology Industries	13	5
Manufacturing Industries	16	4
Total	29	9

HR philosophy, HR efforts directed to goals, human process research, its linkage with other systems, and networking were the dimensions of strategic human resource perspective. it was found that out of 38 organisations, 50 per cent had a proper HR philosophy in place in their organisations, while other 50 per cent were not giving much emphasis on such a philosophy. 18 organisations tried to align HR activities with organisational strategy to make sure that the top management recognises HR efforts in achieving organisational goals. 24 organisations had conducted research to understand human behaviour systems, and 21 organisations tried to link HR system with the other systems of the organisations so that it produces a synergy among the various subsystems for better integration and coordination. 26 organisations had some kind of networking with other professional organisations, agencies, and people for the growth and development of employees, and HR professionals. Thus 19 organisations tried to align their organisational strategy with strategic pespective for developing a fit.

Table 2: Strategic HR Perspective

Dimensions	*HR philo-phy*	*HR efforts directed goals*	*Human with process Research*	*HR linkage with other Systems*	*Network-ing*
Number of IT	11-high	9-high	11-high	9-high	7-high
Industries	7-low	9-low	7-low	9-low	11-low
Number of	8-high	9-high	13-high	12-high	12-high
Manufacturing Industries	12-low	11-low	7-low	8-low	8-low
Total	19-high 19-low	18-high 20-low	24-high 14-low	21-high 17-low	26-high 12-low

High-represents the number of organisations scoring high marks
Low-represents the number of organisations scoring low marks.

HR climate was also measrued to find out the OCTPAC (openness, confrontation, trust, autonomy, pro-action, authenticity, and collaboration) culture prevailing in organisations. It was found that only 4 organisations had excellent HR climate, and 5 organisations had good HR clfimate. 11 organisations had average clfimate, while 18 organisations had below average HR clfimate. These results showed that only few organisations that had good or excellent climate treated people as the most important resource. They also made efforts to develop the competencies in the employees. The management had faith in the capability of people to change. In other organisation, where HR climate was not good, they should make efforts to develop such a culture where people are open, have trust on each other, transparent in their attitude and functions, have healthy confrontation, and collaborate with others to achieve organisational objectives.

It was found that organisations having effective HR practices were better on employee retention, had higher return on assets, constrantly higher profit, and an increase in market share compared to organisations with less effective HR practices. In order to test the various assumptions related to strategic human resource perspectives three major hypotheses were developed under universalistic, contingency and configurational perspective. It was found that effective HR practices led to better organisational practices irrespective of size, technology, and the type of the organisation. Effective HR practices also led to better organisational performance where HR practices were contingent upon organisational strategy. Some configuration of HR practices (between and within) and strategy was related to organisational performance, where HR practices were consistent with organisational strategy. There was no support for the unviersalistic hypothesis that the same HR practices would be effective across all types of organisations.

Organisation with varing financial turnover i.e. small, medium, and large had adopted different sets of HR practices, Similarly, organisations following different types of strategies i.e. prospectors, analyzers, and defenders followed different sets of HR practices. HR practices followed in information technology industry were diffeent compared to manufacturing organisations. Thus, we can say that effective HR practices vary depending upon the organisational strategy, type of industry and their financial turnover.

It was also found that high performing organisations had a positive HR climate compared to low performing organisations. Prospectors fared better and had better organisational climate. Similarly, organisations having positive HR climate had relatively lower employee turnover, higher rate of profit, higher market share, and higher return on assets.

Conclusion

Thus, we can say that strategic HR practices were positive by related with organisational level outcomes in this study. Different sets of HR practices were effective in different types of industry following different types of organisational strategy and varying financial turnover. HRD climate of the organisation had facilitated the implemention of effective HR practices leading to better organisational performance.

REFERENCES

Arthur, J.B. (1992). The linkage between strategy and industrial relations system in American mini-mills. *Industrial and Labour Relations Review*, 45, 488-506.

Bamberger, p. & Phillips, B. (1991). organisational environment and business strategy : Parallel versus conflicting influences on human resource strategy in the pharmaceutical industry. *Human Resource Management*, 30 (1), 153-182.

Becker, B.E. & Husiled, M.A. (1999). Overview of strategic HRM infline leading firms. Human Resource Management, 38, 210-231.

Boreman, C. (1991). Job behaviour, performance, and effectiveness. In M.D. Dunnette and L.M. Plough (Eds.). *Handbook of Industirial and Organisational Psychology*, 2nd Ed., Vol. 2. palo Alto, CA : Consulting Psychologist Press.

Delery, J.E. & Doty, D.H. (1996). Models of theorizing in strategic human resource management : Tests of universalistic, contingency, and configurational performance predictions. *Academy of Management Journal*, 39 (4), 802-835.

Fey, C.F., Bjorkman, I. & Pavlovskaya, A. (2000). The effect of HRM practices on firm performance in Russia. *International Journal of Human Resource Management*, 11, 1-18.

Gratton, C., Hailey, V., & Stiles, P., & Truss, C. (1999). Linking individual performacne to usiness strategy : The people process model. *Human Resource Management*, 38, 28-43.

Guthree, J.P. & Dutta, D.K. (1998). Corporate strategy, executive selection and firm Performance *Human Resource Management*, 37, 12-32.

Harel, G.H. & Tzafrir, S.S. (1999). The effect of HRM practices on the perception of Organisational and market performance of the firm. Human Resource Management, Huselid, M.A., (1995). The impact of human resource management practices on turnover, Productivity, and corporate financial performance. *Academy of Management Journal,* 38, 635-672.

Ichniowski, C., Shaw, K., & Prennushi, G. (1994). The impact of human resource Management practices on productivity. *Columbia Business sChool Working Paper 015,* Columbia University : New York.

Katz, H.C., Kochan, T.A., & Keefe, J.C. (1987). *Industrial Relations and productivity in the U.S. Automobile Industry.* Washington D.C.: Brookings Institute.

Lam, L.W. & White, L.P. (1998). HR orientation and firm performance. Human Resource Development Quarterly, 9, 13-32.

Lengnick - Hall, C.A., & Lengnick-Hall, M.L. (1988). Strategic human resource management : A review of the literature and proposed typology. *Academy of Management REview,* 13, 454-470.

Leonard, J.S. (1990). Executive pay and firm performance. *Industrial and Labour Relations Review,* 43, 13-29.

MacDuffie, J.P. (1995). Human resource bundles and manufacturing performance : Organisational logic and flexible production systems in the world auto industry. *Industrial and Labour Relations Review,* 48, 197-221.

Miles, R.E., & Snow, C.C. (1984). Designing strategic human resource systems. *Organisational Dynbamics,* 13(1), 36-52.

Ostroff, C. (1995). Human resource management: Ideas and trends. *Personnel,* June 21, 356, CCH Incorporated.

Pfeffer, J. (1994) *Competitive Advantage through People: Unleshaing the Power of the Workforce* Harvard Business School Press: Boston.

Rao, T.V. (1999) *HRD Audit: Evaluating the Human REsource Function for Business Improvement.* Response Books, Sage: New Delhi.

Russel, J.S., & Terborg, J.R. & Powers, M.L. (1985). Organisational Performances and Organisational level training and support. *Personnel Psychology,* 23 (2), 156-159.

Scheppeck, M.A. & Miletello, J. (2000). Strategic configuration and Organisational performance. Human Resource Management, 39, 5-16.

SChuler, R.S. (1992). Strategic human resource Management: Linking the people with the Strategic needs of the business. *Organisational Dynamics,* 21(1), 18-32.

Schuler, R.S., & Jackson, S.E. (1988). Linking competitive remuneration practices to Innovation in a competitive strategy. *Human Resource Management Australia,* 10 (May), 6-21.

Tepstra, D.E., & Rozell, E.J. (1993). The relationship of staffing practices to organisational level Measures. *Personnel Pshychology,* 46, 27-48.

Tichey, N.M., Fomburn, C., & Devanna, M. (1982). Strategic human resource management. *Sloan Management Review,* 22 (2), 47-60.

Walker, J.B. (1992). *Human Resource Strategy.* McGraw-Hill: New York.

Weitzman, M.L. & Kruse, D.L. (1990). Profit sharing and Productivity. In Blinder (Ed.).

Paying for Prodicutivity, Washington, D.C.: Brookings Institute.

Yeung, A.K., & Berman, B. (1997). Adding value through human resources : Reorienting Human resource management to drive business performance. *Human Resource Management,* 36(3), 321-335.

3

Population and Food Security in South Asian Perspective

Dr. Falendra K. Sudan

Introduction

In the history of the controversy on the relation of population with economic growth, which began with Malthus, arguments have been advanced on each side, both positive and negative. With large untilised resources and an advanced technology, a big population with a high rate of growth may be considered as an asset, whereas with a poor level of resources and technology, it could be a heavy drag for an economy. In theory, rapid development of technology results in fast rise in productivity, and in such a situation, a high rate of population growth could be so absorbed by the economy as to continuously raise standards of living. In practice, however, the difficulties of achieving rapid expansion of utilisable resources and progress in technology tend to strictly limit the desirable rate of growth of population. It is easy to talk glibly of the population of a country being an asset, which if not productively engaged immediately, turns into a liability. It is an asset that cannot be kept in a frozen state for use at a convenient time like other natural assets of a country. So, it becomes necessary to designate the population as an asset which can be productively employed now or, at most, in a reasonably near future [Sudan (1992)]. Some demographers opine that South Asian countries are unable to feed its present population. Feeding it by the turn of first quarter of the present century will pose a greater problem. South Asian problems of poverty, malnutrition and hunger must be solved by first limiting the population growth and then having equal distribution [Brown (1993); Myres (1991) and Postel (1992)].

The food production capacity of the Earth is high, and has grown substantially in recent times. Since 1970, outputs of crops have doubled and the per capita productions of maize, rice, and wheat have increased over the past 30 years. We produce one fourth more food per capita now than in 1961. Affordability of food is also increasing, as prices have decreased. The gains have occurred both as a result of using more area and more inputs. Extensification has been the norm, mainly through land use conversion, although intensification is now occurring at increasing rates and external inputs are increasing faster than ever. The average yields of most crops are still increasing, although the rates are slowing and are highly variable by location. The net result is that fewer people are hungry now than since the 1960s, when good records began [Hamilton (2000)]. Despite remarkable performance in food production scenario, food insecurity remains a chronic problem [Brklacich, 2000]. Population density in relation to arable land increased considerably since 1950 and is expected to increase further. The population density is less than 100 in South Asia. This, however, does not reveal the whole picture. The density varies from peak above 700 in Bangladesh to the low depths of below 140 in Pakistan [United Nations (1994)]. Since 1950, area of cultivated land per capital has declined significantly. In India, for example, it has dropped from 1.11 acres in 1921 to 0.62 acres in 1971 and a further decline has also been observed in recent past too. In order to counter the decrease in cultivated land per capita and meet the increasing demand for agricultural goods, including food, it is necessary to raise agricultural productivity. From 1900 to 1945, the increase in overall agricultural output was over taken by population increase. In India (then comprising present-day India, Pakistan and Bangladesh), population increased by 18.4 per cent and overall agricultural output increased by 13 per cent [Bhattacharjee (1958)]. In other words, despite the increase in total area under cultivation the agricultural sector did not show any growth. Since mid-1995, growth of food production has been observed to be higher than population growth in all but two. In Bangladesh, these growth rates have been almost the same, but in Nepal the population growth rate has been significantly higher than growth in food production [Sudan (2001)]

If the nutritional level of a given population judges the adequacy of the food supply, South Asia is still a long way from providing the minimum daily requirement of nutritional food. The bulk of South Asian population suffers from general debilitation and lower physical energy and productivity [World Bank (2001)]. The position is worse in respect of nutrient types of food, which are generally outside the reach of the mass of population. Apart from the low level of income, the inability of the people to have sufficient food and a balanced diet is also related to overpopulation. In South Asia, productivity of food grains till recently did not keep pace with the increased demand resulting from population growth and rise in per capita income and, consequently, the prices of food grains rose and the consumption levels of the poorer sections of the society has been depressed. In sum, rapid population growth in South Asia not only affects food production and consumption, but also will profoundly affect the distribution of overall income and assets in the present century. The land tenure patterns, distribution of agrarian incomes and farm holding by size and rates of rural-urban migration is likely to be significantly modified. The rapid population growth seems certain to increase the number of landless, subsistence or disadvantaged peasantry and raise the administrative burdens and social costs of absorbing urban arrivals as well as managing the food aid and assistance. Conversely, the slower population growth could lessen the severity of thse effects, once its cumulative influence on numbers began to take effect.

Malthusian Principle of Population

Malthus was not the first person to suggest that population growth might outstrip the capacity to produce food [Malthus (1798)]. Nor was he the first to suggest that this might limit population size by raising death rates [see Saether (1993); Blaxter (1986)]. But he was certainly most influential and impressive; and modern demographers still frequently acknowledge their debt to him. The basic argument of Malthus' *An Essay on the Principle of Population,* can be sketched with the help of a few famous quotations: "Population, when unchecked, increases in a geometrical [i.e. compound] ratio. Subsistence [i.e. food production] increases only in an arithmetical ratio .... By that law of our nature, which makes food necessary to the life of the man, the effects of these two unequal powers [of population and food] must fall somewhere and must necessarily be severely felt by a large portion of mankind" [Malthus (1798), p. 14] Malthus then proceeded to argue that the balance between population and food is chiefly maintained by upward pressure on the death rate - and that this 'absolutely necessary consequence' was primarily brought about the hunger, starvation and disease. But, should these factors still be insufficient to restore equilibrium, then: "gigantic inevitable famine stalks in the rear, and with one mighty blow levels the population with the food of the world [Malthus (1998), p. 140].

Malthus significantly revised the simple argument on the relationship between population and food of the *First Easay* in his so-called *Second Eassay*. He gave increasing importance to changes in the birth rate as an alternative way of maintaining the balance between 'population' and 'food'. Essentially he argued that when food was scarce and times were hard, prices rose and men and women were forced to delay their marriages. In turn, this reduced the birth rate and helped to restore the equilibrium between population and resources (including food supplies) [Wrigley and Schofield (1981)]. Also, he realised that trade-off could occur. For example, a decline in the birth rate would reduce the risk of a rise in the death rate. Malthus' description of the rate of increase of food production as arithmetic (i.e. linear) was a reasonable generalisation given the evidence that was available to him [Flew (1970)]. He was discussing the increase of food on the implicit assumption that the supply of cropland was fixed. In modern parlance, he was describing the form of growth of agricultural yields-e.g. food output per hectare. During recent decades, the aggregate yields have indeed increased in a fairly linear [Dyson (1996). So, especially the later writings of the Malthus on the adaptabilities, flexibilities and general complexities of the relationship between population and food contain many valuable insights, which are still valid today.

Views of Anti-malthusian

Since Malthus' time there have been periodic 'waves' of people who doubted the capacity of the world to produce enough food for its growing population [Kellman (1987)]. However, so-called 'anti-Malthusian' presented a more optimistic outlook. Instead of seeing a large and growing population as a problem for systems of food production, the opposing perspective sees these characteristics as both a sign and, indeed, a cause of prosperity. According to anti-Malthusian views, the flexibility and adaptability provided by efficient markets through trade can help solve any problems posed by population growth. Indeed, since population growth increases the volume of demand for food, if scarcity occurs then prices will rise and eventually farmers will be stimulated into producing more food. This leads to the view that, over the long run, population growth actually causes food to be both more plentiful and cheaper [Simon (1981)]. Besides markets, scientific research has led to increase in agricultural productivity. Major advances here include the development of mass production techniques for nitrogen fertilizers around 1913, and the development of so-called 'green revolution' high yielding varieties (HYVs) of wheat and rice during the 1960s [Flew (1970)]. The second main way by which farm productivity may be increased is through the stimulation of agricultural innovation induced by population growth itself. Drawing upon African and Asian data Boserup (1965) noted the positive correlation which existed between population density and the intensity of land, use. Societies living at low population densities tended to practise 'extensive' agriculture; farmers would cultivate a plot of land with a few simple tools and then move on to work another patch, letting the original plot lie fallow for perhaps 20-25 years during which time its productivity would recover. Then the rejuvenated plot would be cultivated again. However, societies living at comparatively high population densities were much more likely to cultivate the same plot of land each year (i.e. practise annual cropping). These communities tended to have more sophisticated agricultural systems and farms tools. Moreover, levels of food production per person were sometimes higher under such more 'intensive' farming regimes, particularly if greater inputs of agricultural labour per person were required (i.e. in terms of time spent in cultivation).

From this essentially cross-sectional observation, Boserup argued that through the challenges to society which it posed, population growth often actually worked as the major dynamic engine of agricultural change - stimulating, in particular, the adoption of improvements in land use and technology. Moreover, this basically anti-Malthusian perspective can be further developed to argue that - other things being equal - the larger a population is the larger will be the number of farmers, and therefore the greater will be the chance that someone will discover a new and more productive way of cultivating the available supply of land [Simon (1992) and Boserup (1965)]. There is no doubt that historically such Boserupian processes have been very significant in societies all round the world. Indeed demographic increase may well have been the single most important cause of agricultural intensification. Furthermore, potentially there are many ways in which food production can be increased to keep up with population growth [Bilsborrow (1987)]. No doubt, increased population density may eventually lead to greater intensification, it is not obvious that this will be necessarily be accompanied by increased levels of food production per head. There is widespread agreement among agricultural economists that the innovations which poor farmers in much of the developing world are likely to be able to generate by themselves will be quite incapable of keeping up with such very high rates of population growth [Pingali and Binswanger (1991) and Hayami and Ruttan (1987)]. Indeed, it will be essential to incorporate the benefits of agricultural innovations into the overall processes of adaptive response.

View of Neo-malthusian

The world's population is certainly both larger and better fed now than it was two hundred years ago. In spite of repeated expressions of anxiety, world food production has generally kept ahead of population growth. In large measure this has been due to the more expansion of the area of land in cultivation, plus the continual development of agricultural practices by farmers and, more recently, the application of modern scientific and industrial approaches to the tasks of raising crop yields and transporting and storing food [see Grigg (1993) and Boserup (1990)]. Modern neo-Malthusian writers do not deny that these long-term improvements in per capita food production have taken place. But they argue that in the 1980s and 1990s the world has at last reached a critical turning point. They maintain that in certain crucial respects the situation which humanity now faces is different from that it has confronted in the past. In particular, the neo-Malthusian case highlights the extra ordinary scale of contemporary world population growth and the related-and increasingly serious-environmental problems to which growth contributes. The argument acknowledges that issue of distribution-especially the existence of widespread poverty in much of the developing world, coexistent with over-consumption and waste of resources by rich nations-are very important. But it retains at its core grave anxiety about whether food production can possibly keep up with population growth [see Brown (1993); Brown and Kane (1995); Ehrlich and Ehrlich (1990); Ehrlich *et al.* (1993); and Myres (1991)].

The basic demographic facts underlying the modern neo-Malthusian case are not in dispute. If it took about 130 years for the human population to grow from 1 billion to 2 billion, the next billion were added in just 30 years, i.e. by about 1960. The rate of demographic growth has been declining since 1960s because the world's birth rate has been falling faster than the death rate. But even so, during the 1980s alone the world's population grew by an estimated 841 million people. Moreover, most population projections broadly agree that in the next three decades up to the year 2020, the absolute increment will be about 870 million people in each decade [United Nations (1994)]. The phenomenon of demographic momentum makes most of this growth virtually certain (see McNicoll (1992)]. This unprecedented demographic increase is overwhelmingly located in the developing world where birth rates are the highest and population age structures are youngest. In fact, over 95 per cent of the 2.603 billion increment which the United Nations projects for the period 1990-2020 is expected to occur in the developing countries. This increase in population will be the main cause of a tremendous expansion in the demand for food, and therefore of greatly increased exploitation of land for agricultural production.

At this point environmental considerations and judgements enter the argument and things suddenly become much more complicated. Part of the modern neo-Malthusian case is that food production all over the world is increasingly coming up against various constraints, of which perhaps the two most important relate to land and water. The total amount of cropland is shrinking because of population growth. The greater and greater demands, which are being made upon the land, which is in cultivation, are leading to wisespread land degradation-in such forms as soil erosion, compaction and desertification. It is claimed that throughout much of the developing world mounting population pressures are directly threatening the inherent productivity of the soil [Brown(1988) and Brown and Kane (1995)]. Fast-growing cities are gobbling-up prime agricultural land, and the dwindling supplies of new land which might be brought into cultivation are generally of much poor quality. In case of water, the problems seem to be severe. More than one-third of current world agricultural production is said to come from the approximately 16 per cent of agricultural land that is irrigated. But "Worldwide the prospects for major gains in irrigated area are not good" [Brown (1988)]. So the amount of irrigated cropland per person is also declining because of population growth. Again, there are many difficulties relating to irrigation water than just of falling per capita supplies, which includes rising levels of pollution, increased salinisation of irrigated croplands, falling water tables and increased competition of water - for example between farmers and city-dwellers, and betwen nation states. Furthermore, as is often the case apropos environmental problems, these processes frequently combine and interact in synergistic ways. Fast growing cities threaten supplies of both agricultural land and water. Deforestation of upland areas-often fuelled in part by the migration of poor farmers in search of cultivable land-may cause increased flooding and agricultural destruction downstream. Thus, humanity is confronted with a serious dilemma: a population-environment-food 'trap' [Ehrlich *et al.* (1993)].

The world's population having grown by about 841 million people during the 1980s, the neo-Malthusian case proceeds to argue that these various constraints and threats are already having extremely serious and detectable effects on food production. The 'green revolution' which kept food output ahead of world population growth during the 1960s and 1970s is portrayed as running out of steam. The best locations for planting the high yielding varieties of major cereal crops like rice and wheat have largely been used up. It is contended that many countries have reached the point where higher and higher doses of fertilizer to each hectare of cropland produce very little increase in yields. In lots of places the yields of major food crops are said to be falling, or only increasing slowly [Myers (19910]. According to neo-Malthusian, the 1970s saw increasingly frequent setbacks in the race between population and food. But in the 1980s, there occurred a critical turning point. Since about 1984 the world's population has been growing faster than its production of cereal grains (which form the principal basis of the human food supply). Put differently, since the mid-1980s, the global output of grain per person has been falling [Brown (1993); Brown and Kane (1995); Ehrlich *et al.* (1993); Myres (1991); Population Action International (1992); Postel (1992); and Harrison (1992)]. Furthermore, this negative trend mean that the world's reserve stocks of grain have also been falling. Therefore a couple of exceptionally bad global harvests - arguably more likely under conditions of rapid climate change - could easily cause a repeat of the food prices rises and 'world food crisis' which occurred in the early 1970s [Brown (1988, 1991) and Brown and Kane (1995)]. Beyond this, it is predicted that during the 1990s global agricultural production may grow at an average annual rate of only 0.9 per cent, while population continues growing at around 1.6 per cent. This implies that per capita food production could fall by 7 per cent in the coming decade and raises the prospect of 'an absolute global shortage of food' leading to widespread starvation and famine in developing countries [Enrlich *el al.* (1993) and Brown (1988)]. Thus, the neo-Malthusian view is that in the decades ahead, food shortages will in both frequency and severity. The next ten years could see a major crisis involving 'mounting grain deficits, surging grain prices and spreading hunger among ever larger numbers of people' [Myers (1991); Brown and Kane (1995); Ehrlich and Ehrlich (1990) and Ehrlich *et al.* (1993)]. It is seriously proposed that by 2020 there could be several million excess deaths stemming from hunger and famine [Daily and Ehrlich (1990)].

Some features of the neo-Malthusian argument must be taken more seriously. It would be absurd not to acknowledge that population growth may lead to reduced per capita supplies of cropland and renewable water in the years ahead. It is clear that in many parts of the world rapid demographic growth is contributing to damage the environment, and that this often has adverse consequences for local food production. Furthermore, no one doubts that there will be major growth in global food demand in the next few decades—largely because of population growth. This will certainly present humanity with a considerable challenge. Moreover, certain elements of the neo-Malthusian case can be vaulted comparatively precisely. For example, since the mid-1980s either South Asian population has been growing faster than its cereal production, or it has not. Similarly, either population growth has been outstripping growth of cereal production in all South Asian countries, or it has not. Likewise, either there are signs that famine or food crises are becoming more frequent and severe, or there are not. It is true that these issues are not entirely devoid of judgement. But it is also true that they involve relatively 'hard' and objective sets of data. Moreover, demographic studies can provide us with some comparatively firm indicators as to the likelihood that starvation and famine will curtail South Asian population in the next few decades. By evaluating these rather more specific neo-Malthusian claims, we can get a better idea as to whether the more extreme forecasts deserve any consideration at all.

Situation in South Asia

The South Asian countries, i.e. Bangladesh, India, Nepal, Pakistan and Sri Lanka cover 85 per cent of the region, 96 per cent of the irrigated area, 98 per cent of the population and 99 per cent of the gross domestic product. India is by for the largest country in the region with 72 per cent of land area and 76 per cent of the population. On an average, about 55 per cent of the land area is used for agriculture (including pastures). In Nepal and Sri Lanka, this figure is lower (about 35 per cent). Probably due to the occurrence of mountains. In Pakistan, the low percentage of agricultural land is due to arid conditions. Due to land pressure and flat topography, in Bangladesh almost 80 per cent of the land area is used for agriculture [Roest (2000)]. The arid conditions of Pakistan are reflected in the high percentage of irrigation: almost 80 per cent against 20 to 30 per cent in the other countries of the region. Population growth is highest in Nepal (2.5 per cent), the country with the lowest gross domestic product (together with Bangladesh). Sri Lanka, the most prosperous country, has the lowest population growth of 1.1 per cent [CIA (1998)]. Agriculture as a sector produces about 30 per cent of the gross domestic product in the region, but employees about 65 per cent of the labour force. Remarkably, in all countries the income per capita in agriculture is about 50 per cent of the national average.

Between 1970 and 1990, food supplies in the developing world increased by about 16 per cent and have out placed population growth in most regions. However, food insecurity remains a chronic problem and yield increases are also falling, lessening our ability to meet the growing food needs [Brklacich (2000)]. As recently as the 1970s, South Asia was sub-continent known for its famines and recurrent food crisis. However, during the last two decades, the situation has changed remarkably and increases in food supply remain ahead of population growth in South Asia. At the end of 1998, Pakistan produced its largest ever harvest of wheat at

18.7 million tons. Bangladesh also recorded good cereal harvests, reinforcing its confidence that it might soon attain food self-sufficiency. In 1999, India enjoyed a bumper harvest so large that its warehouses over flowed and food grains were stored under the open sky for lack of space in the go-downs. However, natural disasters worked in opposite direction and jeopardize the food security scenario in most parts of the region. In 2000, drought devastated agriculture and industry in India and Pakistan. A super-cyclone ravaged India's state of Orissa and staturated more than 1 million hactares of cropland [WFP (2002)].

The Indian sub-continent is two thirds larger in population than the entire continent of Africa. The population densities in the region are high: one out of five people live in the region [World Bank (2001)]. With about 294 million classified by the FAO as undernourished (over 200 million people in India alone), the region has significant problems related to food security [FAO (2000)]. Cereals represent a high share of dietary intake, ranging from 57 per cent in Pakistan to 83 per cent in Bangladesh. In 1997, South Asia produced 29 per cent of the world's rice, 15 per cent of the world's wheat and 11 per cent of the world's oil crop [FAOSTAT (2000)]. Most South Asian countries are net importers of wheat and about 6.4 million tons of wheat is imported annually (6.6 per cent of the world wheat trade during 1996-98). During the recent past, India and Pakistan have emerged as net exporters of rice: India exported 3.1 million tons while Pakistan exported 1.8 million tons during 1996-98. All other countries in the region are importers of rice the largest being Bangladesh at 1.3 million tons. With the exception of Nepal, each of the countries imports pulses to meet national requirements. During 1996-98, the annual average imports amounts to 8.1 per cent of the pulses production in the region [FAO (2000)].

Based on FAO food balance sheets, dietary energy supply per capita is generally higher than it was in 1970.

However, in Bangladesh, it has dropped by 4.5 per cent. In Sri Lanka, a decline in dietary energy supply per capita, at the beginning of the 1980s coincides with the resurgence of violence in that country. It is important to note that despite relative prosperity in the country, Sri Lanka's dietary energy supply per capita is the lowest in the region, followed by Bangladesh. Taking 1995 as a benchmark the average dietary energy supply per capita was 73 per cent of the developed world's dietary energy supply (2329) kcal versus 3207 kcal). Normally, standards of adequacy can be achieved only at national calorie supply levels of about 2800 kcal per capita per day (2700 kcal per person per day, is estimated by FAO (1996b), and only if the national food distribution is relatively equalitarian and public health services work satisfactory [Fogel (1997)]. All the countries in the region are classified as low income, food deficit country, which suggest a priority status for development assistance under WFP food resource allocation decisions. Gross national product (GNP) per capita in the region ranges from US$ 210 in Nepal, US$ 350 in Bangladesh, over US$ 400 in India and Pakistan to over US$ 800 in Sri Lanka. Economic growth rates also vary enormously, from a low of 2 per cent in Nepal to a robust 6 per cent per annum in India [World Bank (2001)]. In the following paragraphs, a separate account has been given with regard to the food production and availability.

In Bangladesh, all governmental plans have consistently emphasized the achievement of food self-sufficiency. Although the country has not experienced a famine since 1974, food, and the fear of not having enough, plays a crucial role in the agriculture-led political economy of Bangladesh [Ahmed et al. (2000)]. Green revolution technologies introduced after in dependence in the 1970s as well as far-reaching market-oriented agricultural reforms undertaken during the late 1980s and early 1990s, led to sustained growth in rice production. Much of the expansion came from a shift from traditional varieties to modern high yielding one, increased application of fertilizer, and through an expansion of cropped area during the dry season by irrigation. The accompanying reforms comprised considerable deregulation of agricultural markets and prices, such as fertilizers, seeds, and irrigation; and gradual cutbacks of the subsidized food rationing system and public procurement of grains. The growth in grain production stagnated in the early 1990s registering less than one percent annual growth rate during 1990-97, compared to 2.8 per cent in the 1970s and about 4 per cent in the 1980s. During this period, there were growing doubts about Bangladesh's ability to increase food production to 31 million tons, its projected requirement by 2010. However, several successive bumper harvests (in the late 1990s) have reinforced its confidence that food self-sufficiency is possible in the near future [WFP (2001)].

Overall, the strategy of cereal self-sufficiency has been quite successful, from producing only 11 million tons in 1970, cereal production nearly doubled to over 21 million tons in 1999 [FAOSTAT (2000)]. Parellel to the increase in food production, food imports dropped from 26 to 30 per cent of total import volume and 50 to 70 per cent of export earnings in the 1980s, to 18 per cent of all imports and 34 per cent of Bangladesh's total export earnings in recent years. In the 1990s, Bangladesh's annual food-grain imports have been in the range of 1-2.5 million tons. However, hikes tend to occur in response to 'disaster year', such as in 1988, 1991, or 1998. When cereal imports increased due to the relief measures that were implemented following widespread floods or major cyclones [WFP (2000)]. Rice imports, for example, reached up to 2.6 million tons in the disaster year of 1998. Despite the impressive increase in domestic production, Bangladesh have still the lowest dietary energy supply per capita in the region. Making the situation worse, the prevalent consumption pattern indicates that the national diet is nutritionally extremely unbalanced, with cereals making up an astonishingly high 82 per cent [FAOSTAT (2000)].

Bangladesh's proneness to disaster is a key risk factor for the national food economy and for household food security. As has happened recurrently in the past, disasters wipe out crops and cause immense damage to the physical and social infrastructure. Incorporating disaster mitigation into development policies and programmes is an absolute imperative, more than in any other country of the region. Another impending food insecurity factor is urbanization like other countries in South Asia, Bangladesh's rapidly growing urban population will not to be fed, and pressures on the government to control food prices may have a major effect on reforms in its agricultural and food assistance policies.

Over the last 50 years, India has made significant strides in its food grain production. Its output has increased from about 55 million tons to over 2000 million tons, an increase of 263 per cent. During the same period, the population grew from 360 million to above 1000 million (188 per cent increase). This success is attributed in part to the Green Revolution that started in the late 1960s and was characterized by huge public investments in irrigation infrastructure and research, land reforms, introduction of high-yielding varieties of seeds and the expanded use of fertilizer and pesticides. The new agricultural technologies pushed up productivity of wheat and rice. However, the benefits of the "green revolution" were unequally distributed among the farmers. The 'winners' were primarily wheat producers with large and medium landholding under irrigation in the north-west namely in Punjab and Haryana. In the 1980s, India became self-sufficient in food grains and a marginal net-exporter, During that period the average production growth rate was 3.5 per cent per annum [Haller (1999)]. Like Bangladesh, India could not maintain this pace. Food grain output grew at a rate only 1.8 per cent per annum, a slightly higher than the growth rate of population (1.7 per cent). Moreover, the huge growth in food grain output since the 1960s was based on just two crops; wheat and rice. The annual growth of production of pulses remained more of less stangnant during last 30 years and coarse cereal production actually declined [FAOSTAT (2000)].

Currently, India's macro availability dimension of food security is premised on self-sufficiency in wheat and rice and on net imports of pulses and vegetable oil. Imports of cereals no longer play a significant role given the sheer size of India's domestic production. Since 1990s, India has been twice a net importer of food grain. The trade liberalisation had a significant impact in certain agricultural sub-sectors. For instance, domestic production of pulses and vegetable oil has been either stagnant or declining, the trade liberalisation in the 1990s has resulted in considerable gain in imports market share, between 20 and 30 per cent of domestic production [FAOSTAT (2000)]. This has increased the availability of oil and lower prices in the local market. The large-scale dependence on imports could be dangerous to India, given the food grain supply and demand compared to the international cereal market. The current level of consumption is 175 million MT, whereas the country produces 190 million MT cereals, and the size of world cereal market is about 250 million MT. The dependence on imports would make the country vulnerable to the international price fluctuations and price hikes. In the extreme, situations could arise where the world market supply of food grains cannot meet the domestic demand. Over the period, considerable gains in food availability have been made, this has not resulted in an equitable distribution of food in all parts of the country due to infrastructural constraints, market imperfections, and governmental regulations, resulting in regional food scarcities. The increase in population and changing consumption pattern due to rising incomes and progressive urbanisation will influence the future food demand. The total demand for food grains will range from 250 to 360 million tons to feed a population of 1.2 billion by 2010 [Bhalla et al. (1999)]. The future challenges for India includes both raising food output and ensuring sustainable, stable, and widely shared growth in food supplies. The larger food supplies must also come from rising biological yields and the replacement of chemical fertilizers with bio-fertilizers, besides area expansion and more irrigation which calls for heavy investment in research, bio-technology development and its dissemination. Keeping the rising income levels, India will be facing a herculean task if it wants to meet the rising demand from domestic production.

Nepal is an overwhelmingly agrarian economy, with agriculture contributing more than 40 per cent to the GDP, the highest share of all South Asian countries [Mahbub UL Haq Human Development Centre (2000)]. Nepal has shifted from a position of national food grain surpluses to chronic food deficits. In the early 1980s, Nepal still has net trade surplus in rice, but since the early 1990s, food imports have increased substantially. Today, 45 out of 75 districts are considered food deficit. During the recent past, the overall agricultural growth rate of 2.2 per cent has not kept pace with population growth (2.4 per cent), which can be attributed to land degradation due to extremes in precipitation, marginal soil and serious erosion of agricultural top-soil, dwindling forest resources, and irrigation constraints [WFP (2001)]. One of the most crucial factors affecting food accessibility and availability is the lack of communication and transport infrastructure [Mathema (1999)]. An escalating domestic insurgency in many remote mid-hill and mountain districts has had an impact on the food security of the regions. The intensification of agriculture in the *Tarai,* and the diversification of its agriculture in the hills and mountains will be the key to Nepal's food security in the coming decades. There is urgent need for making heavy investment in the road infrastructure in order to open up remote areas, i.e., the areas of acute food insecurity. Alongside the roads, much can be done for food insecure household to help them transform their agricultural practices from unsustainable subsistence pattern to more profitable approaches such as community forestry, agro-forestry, and cash cropping. In Nepal, the future food security is linked to how well it meets this redistribution challenge.

In Pakistan, the breakthrough in agriculture came with the green revolution in the 1960s, with the subsidized supply of new seeds and fertilisers and the increase in water availability, both through canal and tube well irrigation. As a result, agriculture grew by more than 4 per cent per annum in the 1960s, fell to 2.6 per cent in the 1970s, but again picked up in the 1980s. This partly offset the discrimination against agriculture. However, as in other South Asian countries, the impact and benefits of the green revolution were confined mainly to regions with extensive irrigated areas (Punjab, Sindh and parts of NWFP0, and the dissemination of the technology package was biased in favour of the large farmers [Islam (1996)]. Today, Pakistan's agricultural economy is characterized by self-sufficiency in cereal production and exports of high quality rice and cotton. More than two-thirds of the overall cereal production of 23 million MT is wheat. Despite sustained growth in production, Pakistan has to import 2 to 2. million tons wheat per annum to feed its population, which is growing at a persistently high rate of 2.8 per cent (the highest in South Asia). Oilseed production in Pakistan represents another notable setback, from a position of self-sufficiency, the country has now become a net-importer. Efforts to expand the production of non-traditional oilseeds have failed as domestic price policies and wide scale imports of cheap foreign cooking oils have effectively curbed production incentives [WFP (2001)].

A strong focus on sustainable increase in domestic food production might be necessary considering the country's increasing difficulties in financing food imports. Since the mid-1990s, Pakistan faced slow economic growth, rapid inflation, declining foreign exchange reserves, and large fiscal deficits. High and increasing imports of wheat and oil have worsened Pakistan's chronic balance of payments deficits and foreign exchange shortages. All this has led to increases in prices of food. Like India, agriculture sector in Pakistan has a large potential for growth, and for most crops, the yield gap between current and potential yields is significant. To what extent this gap can be closed depends upon the ability of the country to address the challenges in the agriculture sector. Less optimistic food production projection based on the past trends suggest serious shortfalls in food grains, which will increase from over four million tons in 2000 to over ten million tons by 2025. The future food security in Pakistan will depend on both its natural resource endowments and its policy framework. While Pakistan has sufficient land resources to produce enough food to meet the entire domestic demand, its key constraint is water. Once considered a water-rich country, today Pakistan is in the midst of a growing water crisis. This affects primarily the irrigation system, which currently uses 97 per cent of the water. Cropping patterns have been based on the false premise of abundant water. Pakistan's canal irrigation network was designed in the midst of the green revolution to support cropping intensity of only 70 to 80 per cent annually, with thinly spread supplies for a thinly spread population growth and consequent land fragmentation, combined with low crop yields, have forced the farmers to double their cropping intensity well beyond the design assumptions of the infrastructure. Another determinant of Pakistan's future food security will be closely connected to political and economic developments. In the past, food insecurity has been less an issue due to good marketing network and generalised wheat subsidies. However, latest data suggests that these subsidies still required over US $ 200 million of government funds (Pasha et al (2000)], have now been terminated. From the perspective of the local food producers, this is a positive step because sustainable increases in food production will require non-distorted food markets. But poor households would suffer, if the macro food security instruments of the past were dropped without any substitute. The newly planned 'National Food Programme' that targets poor families, would be a step in the right direction.

Sri Lanka has a comparatively high degree of food security compared to its other South Asia neighbours. However, in certain areas, its food economy is precarious. Sri Lanka's biggest food security concern is the on-going civil conflict and its impact on vulnerable population. As many as one million people have been displaced by the war, with more than 680,000 fed by the government in 'welfare camps' waiting for the fighting to stop so that they can return home and resume their lives [WFP (1999)]. In addition to the massive economic and property damage caused by the war, food production has also suffered. The north and east of Sri Lanka were major producers of both crops and fish, and production of these has been greatly affected. The second national food security concern is the country's so-called 'dry-zone'. This zone is less densely populated than other parts of Sri Lanka and is rainfed or under minor irrigation; and agriculturally much less diversified than the water region of the country. The main crop produced in the dry zone is paddy. But production costs are high and cheaper imports, for example, from India, are increasing the pressure for major structural changes. Sri Lanka has been a net importer of food and the major proportion of the Sri Lankan diet is imported. The government has taken steps to promote local food production, especially rice. Numerous irrigation projects have increased the amount of land under cultivation (from 340,000 ha in 1948 to 750,000 ha in 1998), which along with the introduction of green revolution technologies have increased yields from 1.4 to 3.5 tons per hectare. Nevertheless, compared to its neighbour, India, Sri Lanka is a high cost producer of rice. As the economy continues its structural transformation, the emphasis on rice production is likely to diminish, especially if regional free trade opens agricultural markets to more competition.

Conclusions

Overall, the application of green revolution technologies in South Asian countries have resulted into greater food security and made food economies more resilient to famine. However, projections suggest that South Asia could face increasing food insecurity during the current decade, as the amount of food needed to maintain consumption at current levels could increase steeply depending on factors such as population growth, a slowdown in the growth in grain cultivation area, and the influence of rising incomes on dietary composition. Pakistan is projected to have the highest status quo food gap. India still has potential for food grain production increases, especially in the North-Eastern states. To a lesser extent, also Bangladesh can squeeze more output from its land with improved agro-technology. Although Bangladesh will continue to import wheat, the country is perched on the edge of rice self-sufficiency. By contrast, Pakistan faces a resource crunch. Its limits to growth relate to water supplies, despite of broad irrigation coverage. The Himalayan Kingdom of Nepal do not has have potential for irrigation that India, Pakistan, and Bangladesh have. Nepal's comparative advantage lies in exploiting upland-lowland interaction and trade. Given the extreme bio-diversity, country has greater potential for growing high value cash crops; and rural accessibility, in terms of both communication and market integration, is a key issue. Sri Lanka has very different food economy than the rest of the region. Sri Lanka's plantation sector with its high degree of export-orientation is an important element of the food economy. With its large earnings from trade, it has been able to import sufficient supplies of basic commodities. Thus, the country-wise food security scenario in South Asia varies greatly. The answer to expected future food insecurity problem lies in strengthening existing food based interventions that have long been instrumental in mitigating the worst effects of access and utilization failure among the poorest household.

South Asia has been the recipient of vast quantities of international food aid over the past five decades. It has also been implementing some of the largest and most ambitious national food assistance programmes in the world. There is no doubt that such intervention since 1950s saved millions of people from starvation.

REFERENCES

1. Ahmed, R.,S. Haggblade and T.-e-E. Chowdhury (eds.) (2000), *Out of the Shadow of Famine: Evolving Food Markets and Food Policy in Bangladesh,* Johns Hopkins University Press/ International Food Policy Research Institute, Baltimore.
2. Bhalla, G.S., Peter Hazell and John Kerr (1999), *Prospects for India's Cereal Supply and Demand to 2020,* Food, Agriculture, and the Environment, Discussion Paper No. 29, International Food Policy Research Institute, Washington, D.C.
3. Bhattacharjee, j.P. (ed.) (1958), *Studies in indian Agricultural Economics,* Bombay, cited in Sudan, F.K., *Demographic Transition in South Asia,* Anmol Publication, 1992.
4. Bilsborrow, R.E. (1987), 'Population Pressures and Agricultural Development in Developing Countries: A conceptual Framework and Recent Evidence', *World Development Vol.* 15, No. 2, p. 183-203.
5. Blaxter, K. (1986), *People, Food and Resources,* Cambridge University Press, Cambridge.
6. Boserup, E. (1965), *The Conditions of Agricultural Growth,* George Allen and Unwin, London.
7. Boserup, E. (1990), *Economic and Demographic Relationships in Development,* Johns Hopkins University Press, Baltimore.
8. Brklacich, Mike (2000), "Food Security", *IHDP Update,* No. 2, Bonn, Germany.
9. Brown, L.R. ((1988), 'The Changing World Food Prospect: The Nineties and Beyond', *Worldwatch Paper 85,* Worldwatch Institute, Washington, D.C.
10. Brown, L.R. (1991), The New World Order', in L.R. Brown, C. Flavin and S. Postel (eds) *State of the World 1991,* Earthscan Publications Ltd., London.

11. Brown, L.R. (1993), A New Era Unfolds' in L.R. Brown, C. Flavin and S. Postel (eds) *State of the World 1993,* W.W. Norton, New York.

12. Brown, L.R. and Kane, H. (1995), Full House: Reassesssing the Earth's Population Carrying Capacity, Earthscan Publications Ltd., London.

13. CIA (1998), *The CIA World Fact Book, 1998.*

14. Daily, G.C. and Elrlich, P.R. (1990), 'An Exploratory Model of the Impact of Rapid Climate Change on the World Food Situation', *Proceedings of the Royal Society of London, B 241,* p. 232-44.

15. Dyson, T. (1991), 'On the Demography of South Asian Famines, Part II', *Population Studies,* Vol. 45, No. 2, p. 279-97.

16. Dyson, T. (1996), *Po-pulation and Food: Global Trends and Future Prospects,* Routledge, London and New York.

17. Ehrlich, P.R. (1986), *The Population Bomb,* Ballantine Books, New York.

18. Ehrlich, P.R. and Ehrlich, A. H. (1990), *The Population Explosion,* Simon B. Schuster, New York.

19. Ehrlich P.R. and Ehrlich, A.H. and Daily, G.C. (1993), 'Food security, population and the Environment', *Population and Development Review,* Vol. 19, No. 1, p. 1-32.

20. FAO (1983), *Report of the Eighth Session of the Committee on World Food Security,* CL 83/10, Rome.

21. FAO (1992), 'World Food Supplies and Prevalence of Chronic Under-Nutrition in Developing Regions and Assessed in 1992', Document ESS/MISC/1/92, Food and Agriculture Organisation, Rome.

22. FAO (1996), *Rome Declaration on Food Security and World food Summit Plan of Action,* Rome.

23. FAO(2000), *New Dimensions in Water Security,* United Nations, Rome.

24. FAOSTAT (2000), Online FAO Statistical Database - *http://apps.fao.org,* Rome.

25. Flew, A. (ed.) (1970), Malthus, T. R. *An Essay on the Principle of Population and a Summary View of the Principle of Population, Penguin,* Harmondsworth.

26. Fogel, Robert (1997), 'The Global Struggle to Escape from Chronic Malnutrition since 1700,' *Ending the Inheritance of Hunger*, World Food Programme, United Nations University Seminar, Rome: World Food Programme.

27. Grigg, M. (1993), *The World Food Problem*, 2nd edn, Basil Blackwell, Oxford.

28. Haller, A. (1999), 'National Food Surpluses and Food Aid in India,' *Mimeo*, Worls Food Programme, Regional Office for South Asia, New Delhi.

29. Harrison, P. (1992), *The Third Revolution: Environment, Population and a Sustainable World*, I. B. Tauris, London.

30. Hayami, Y. and Ruttan, V. R. (1987), 'Population Growth and Agricultural poverty', in D. G. Johnson and R. D. Lee (eds) Population Growth and economic Development: Issues and Evidence, University of Wisconsin Press, Madison.

31. Islam, Nurul, (1996), 'Growth, Poverty and *Human Development: Pakistan', Human Development Report Office, Occasional Paper 31*, New York: United Nations Development Programme, New York.

32. Kellman, M. (1987), *Word Hunger, A Neo-Malthusian Perspective*, Praegrt, New York.

33. Krishnaji, N. and T. N. Krishnan (2000), *Public Support for Food Security: The Public Distribution System in India, Sage Publications*, New Delhi.

34. Mahbub Ul Haq Human Development Centre (2000), *Human Development in South Asia*, 2000, Oxford University press, Karachi.

35. Malthus, T. R. (1798), *An Essay on the Principle of Population as it Affects the Future Improvement of Society with Remarks on the Speculations of Mr. Godwin, M. condoecet, and Other writers*, St Paul's Church-yard, London.

36. Malthus T. R. (1830/1970), *A Summary View of the Principle of Population*, John Marray, London, reprinted in A. Flew (ed) (1970), Malthus T. R., *An Essay on the Principle of Population and a Summary View of the Principle of Population*, Penguin, Hormondsworth.

37. Mathema, Sudarshan B. (1999), 'Strategy of Sustainable Rural Livelihoods and Social Exclusion for nepal: A Review of the

Literature,' *Mimeo*, Department for International Development, Kathmandu.

38. McNicoll, G. (1992), 'The United Nations' Long Range Population Projections', *Population and Development Review* Vol. 18, No. 2, p. 333-40.
39. Myers, N. (1991), *Population, Resources and the Environment: The Critical Challgnge*, United Nations Population Fund, New York.
40. Pasha, H. A., S. Jafarey and H. R. Lohano, (2000), "Evaluation of Social Safety Nets in Pakistan," *Research Report*, No. 32, Social Policy and Development Centre, Islmabad.
41. Pingali, P. and Binswanger, H. P. (1991), 'Population Dewnsity and Farming Systems', in R. D. Lee, W. B. Arthur, A. C. Kelley, G. Rodgers and T. N. Srinivasan (eds) Population, Food, and Rural Development, Clarendon Press, Oxford.
42. Population Action International (1992), Population and the Environment: impact in the Developing World, Population Action International, Washington, D.C.
43. Postel, S. (1992). "Water for Food Production in South Asia: An Overview of ICID Draft Country Papers," In Mollinga Peter P. (ed.), *Water for Food and Rural Development: Approaches and Initiatives in South Asia*, Sage Publications: New Delhi.
45. Saether, A. (1993), 'Otto Diederich Lutken: 40 years before Malthus?', *Population Studies*, Vol. 47, No. 3, p. 511-13.
46. Simon, J.L. (1981), *The Ultimate Resource*, Martin Robertson, Oxford.
47. Simon, J.L. (1992) *Population and Development in Poor Countries, Selected Essays*, Princeton University Press, Princeton.
48. Sudan, F.K. (1992), *Demographic Transition in South Asia*, Anmol Publication, New Delhi.
49. Sudan, F.K. (2001), Water Scarcity and Food Security: Some policy Issues, Paper contributed for Second Biennial Conference of India Society for Ecological Economics, at Indian Institute of Forest Management, Bhopal, during Dec. 2001.
50. United Nations (1994), *World Population Prospects: The 1994 Revision—Annex Tables*, United Nations, New York.
51. World Bank, (1986), *Poverty and Hunger, Issues and Options for Food Security*, Washington, D.C., USA.

52. World Bank, (2001), *World Development Report, 2000-2001*, Oxford University Press, New Delhi.

53. World Food Programme (WFP) (1999), Assistance to Internally Displaced People. Country case Study on Internal Displacement—Sri Lanka, Displacement in the North and East, Rome.

54. World Food Programme (WFP) (2000), *Food Aid Flows to SAARC*, 1987-99 REgional Office for South Asia, New Delhi.

55. World Food Programme (WFP) (2001). *Enabling Development: Food Assistance in South Asia*, Oxford University Press, New Delhi.

56. Wrigley, E.A. and Schofield, R.S. (1981), *The Population History of England 1541-1871: A REconstruction* Edward Arnold, London.

4

The Status of Women Work Force

Dr. P. Sivaprakasam
R. Suriakala

Women, a weaker and oppressed section, are an important segment of the Indian society. The neglect and discrimination of women in India are well-known. She belongs to the vulnerable part of the Indian society as she sleeps last and rises first. She feeds her family first and eats last. She is the last to receive education and first to drop out of it. She is the last to get a proper job and the first to be laid off during "structural adjustment". She is the last to be consulted for decisions about her environment and the first to be affected[1].

Male superiority and female inferiority are accepted social norms in India. Female inferiority and dependence emanate from the social belief that woman is physically weak, intellectually poor, mentally inconsistent, timid and irrational and psychologically unstable. It is also believed that a woman cannot exist except under constant protection and supervision of a man who is supposed to be physically strong, assertive, rational, intelligent and calculative. Hence, it is often felt that marriage is the only option open to women. Within the marriage framework, the husband and his family control all outside relationships. Women are dependent on the goodwill of their husbands and most often they have no independent financial standing.

However, the heavy demands like dowry set by the bridegroom's party have made marriage a nightmare for many parents. Families with unmarried daughters are looked down by the society. Dowry is paid at the time of marriage but demands continue even after the marriage. Failure to meet the demands could mean physical and mental violence for the woman. Dowry deaths are "normal" occurrences in Indian society. Hence, more women opt for jobs not only to support their parents before marriage but to become self-reliant even after their marriage.

Constitutional Provisions

The constitutional provisions today make it clear that women have equal rights with men in all spheres of life. The age-old suppression of women by men has been put to an end atleast constitutionally. Women are free like men to choose any form of education and training to equip themselves for a career. The constitution not only gives equality in education to women but it also assures equal opportunity to women in matters of public appointments. It says, "there shall be equality of opportunity for all citizens in matters relating to employment or appointment to any office under the state and no citizen shall, on grounds only of religion, race, caste, sex, place of birth, residence or any of these, be ineligible for or discriminated against in respect of any employment or office under the state"[2]. Plans and programmes should be formulated not merely to educate women for new responsibilities and provide them with opportunities for employment in public life, but also to promote an entirely new set of attitudes and values concerning the role and status of women.

Women as Work-forece

Women are taking up jobs due to various reasons. A few women work as sole supporters of the family while others work as additional bread-winners of the family.

Women face lots of problems in seeking employment. The Report of the National Committee on the Status of Women (1975)[3], pointed out that the statutory provision of maternity benefits and welfare facilities like creches and separate sanitary conveniences constituted a negligible expenditure to the establishments. Similarly the private establishments, by and large, have stopped recruiting women as they argue that when there is a choice between an equally competent man and woman, why should not they prefer a man who could not be needing maternity leave and would not present his employers with the above said problem[4].

Studies have shown that many times, a number of industrial organisations do advertise for the post or posts exclusively meant for male applicants. Studies have also shown that when women apply for traditionally male jobs, they tend to get rejected at the initial stage of selection by screening and shortlisting of job applications. In case they are called for an interview either by mistake or otherwise, they, in general, tend to get lower evaluation in the selection process[5].

Inspite of these factors, Indian women are compelled to seek employment due to many reasons. The Ministry of Labour, Government of India[6] has pointedout that whatsoever is the stage of economic or social development of a country, four factors prevail which lead women to join the work force. They are : Inadequate income of the principal earner which forces women to work and supplement the income; mishaps such as incapacity of the bread-winner death of the bread winner and a woman's desire for economic independence or for securing a higher standard of living. There is also a desire on the poart of the woman to give expression to her own talents and skills. Some other studies have brought to light the fact that loneliness is a powerful motive for women to seek employment outside their homes.

Nowadays, their importance as a work-force has been either neglected or misrepresented especially in developing nations. Many activities of women in economically gainful work are either given no recognition or not properly represented in the statistical data. Even if they get employment after undergoing all the hurdles, they are made to abide by the traditional perception of male-female relationship. They find it difficult to interact as they have been trained to listen, obey and leave decision-,making to men in the family or in the business situation. It is also felt that they pose special problems to their employers because of their high absenteeism and turnover by rejecting promotions and resisting transfers[7].

Dual Role of Women Employees

The new role of women of sharing in the income-earning acjtivity has come to co-exist with their primary status as mothers and housewives. Women's occupational status is closely associated with the home and the family. A clear conflict emerges between the socially approved status of women as home-maker on the one hand and status as an employed worker on the other. Familial duties come in the way of employment prospects. Women face the dilemma of somewhat contradictory role perceptions. The loyalties, interests and aims differ betwen home and work place which demand two different types of individualities. When a housewife takes the working role, she not only finds a change in her status within the family and outside it, but she also takes upon herself increasing peressures to reconcile the dual burden of the two roles located in different sectors of the society, in house and work-place. Women employment implies two things: her diminished availability to others and increased demand placed upon others to enable successful performance of her two roles[8].

Status of Women Employment in India and Abroad

Women make up nearly 50 per cent of the world's population, comprise 33 per cent of the official labour force, perform about 70 per cent of the official labour force, pefrom about 70 per cent of all working hours, receive 10 per cent of world's income and own less than 1 per cent of world's property[9]. The statistics show the real position of women in the world. It has also been observed that women have been subjected to under-education, explioitation and social castigation. Discrimination too prevails in offering employment opportunities to women in India. With all the difficulties in estimation, the number of women in the unorgansed sector is many times more than that in the organised sector. The employment in unorganised sector is not felt worthy in most cases as it is not governed by Minimum Wages Act, 1948; Factories Act, 1948; Contract Labour (Regulation and Abolition)Act, 1979 and the like[10]. Hence, it offers no guarantee of minimum wages or security of tenure or gratuity or pension or paid leave. There are so many other problems that are vested with the unorganised sector - legal rights of the workforce are much weaker and unions virtually absent. Women in the unorganised sector have no benefits at all and often have to work for long hours and even no night shifts. Here, their domestic role is completely and deliberately ignored. The modification in the industrial scenario, because of the new economic policies framed by the Government, also hits the women employment to a large extent[11].

Organised sector includes all public sector establishments and private sector establishments employing 10 persons or more[12]. The number of women employed in this sector increased from 1.37 millions in 1962 to 2.14 millions in 1973, that is, an increase of 56.2 per cent[13]. According to 1990 census, women going to employment was 22.27 per cent while men 51.6 per cent. Women employed in central government services constitute 7.5 per cent while in public sector undertakings it was 12.8 per cent. Women occupying managerial positions in America was 42.7 per cent, in Italy 53.8 per cent whereas in India it was 2.3 per cent[14]. Out of total estimated employment of 26.8 million in the organised sector, only 3.8 million are women constituting around 14 per cent only. Even among all working women, only 4 per cent are in the organised sector and 96 per cent are in the unorganised sector[15]. Quite an extensive opportunity is provided to women in an informal sector which is considered to be largely unprotected and outside the realm of policy making[16].

Senior key executive positions are not offered to women eventhough women are remarkably similar to men in their characteristics, abilities and motives[17]. The deep-rooted belief that women are shy, insecure, docile and lack leadership qualities is to be eradicated[18] and it should be understood that traits like confidence, determination, hardwork and boldness which are necessary for career women are well-possessed by present-day women of India.

Here an attempt is made to understand the conditions of employment for women in other countries. The Government of Bagladesh encourages women to enter public service through a quota system, that is, 10 per cent of grade 1 - 10 (gazetted posts) and 15 per cent of posts in grades 11-20 (non-gazetted posts). However, the reality is that there were insufficient women to fill these posts. The main reason was the lack of sufficient technical education to enable them to compete for these positions[19]. In Maldives, though job opportunities are provided for women, moving out of their homes for employment in an industry, has not always been positively entertained by the womenfolk. With the decline in the ratio of women in the labour force, men account for over 80 per cent of total persons employed, as shown in the 1980 census[20]. The participation of women in the industrial sector in Nepal remains low at 1.2 per cent. Women are engaged in spinning, weaving, knitting, carpet making etc. Lack of education, training, mechanical knowledge and supervisory skills all mean that women enjoy less opportunities in interesting and better remunerated jobs[21].

To many middle class women in the Western hemisphere, the women's movement signifies liberation mainly from sexual oppression and secondary status; to be free from the traditional familial roles and duties assigned to women by virtue of their sex. They do not wish to remain being just a wife, a mother or a homemaker. They want to pursue creative or professional activities or aim for social, economic and intellectual achievements. These activities provide them with outlets for individual expression as well as sources of personal satisfaction. In general, their demand for freedom is aimed at achieving recognition of worth as an individual. Thus, it can be seen that an increasing number of women have also become economically active in Asian Countries like Japan, Philippines, Malaysia and Srilanka. In contrast, the Middle East has very low rates of female labour force participation[22].

Plights of Women Employees

(i) A few studies about women employees reveal that their distribution across different categories is quite uneven. A very few women employees happen to be in the officer cadre whereas almost 28 per cent of male employees are in the officer cadre; 50 per cent of male employees are clerks while 83 per cent of female employees occupy this cadre[23].

(ii) Many married women employees have to seek transfer to their husband's place of posting, if their husbands work elsewhere. If this is not possible they are forced to quit their jobs in order to join their husbands.

(iii) A working mother is often forced to take leave so as to rear her children. If her child is three to four years old it can be left in a creche or in the care of grand parents. But similar problem would arise on the arrival of the next

child. A larger number of high potential women are forced to forego promotions and continue as clerks in order to raise their children.

(iv) Gaps in service also disturb the career growth of women. Since the patriarchal family structure is largely intact today inspite of women's higher status, they have to fulfill all the duties concerning the household. Hence, they often have to forego their seniority due to long breaks. The other factors which hinder the career growth are the limitations arising out of spatial immobility, transferable nature of husband's job and educational deprivation which also forces women to confine themselves to stereotyped, low paid, less prestigious and insecure jobs[24].

(v) Since promotions to higher cadre entails transfer, it poses a threat to the harmonious family life of women employees. Hence, large number of bright and competent women decide to sacrifice their career ambitions and opt against promotions so that their family life is not disturbed[25].

(vi) Trade Unions are also indifferent to the problems of women. An agenda for negotiations between unions and bank managements show that women related issues are not raised by unions for negotiations[26].

(vii) Men are reluctant to include women in their non-work conversations and informal discussions. As a consequence of social isolation whether imposed by others or inflicted by self, working women experience an intense feeling of loneliness. Thus, female

employees are significantly more alienated than their male counterparts.

Women Work Force Development Schemes and Programmes

A series of laws have been enacted from time to time to raise the status of women[27]. The First Five Year Plan formulated measures for women and the Central Welfare Board under the Department of Social and Women's Welfare was established in 1953. The second Five Year Plan suggested speedy implementation of the principle of equal pay for equal work and stated that women should be protected against injurious work and should receive maternity benefits and creches for children. The plan periods also saw the enactment of important specific legislations like the Equal Remuneration Act, 1976. The Sixth Plan document stated that one of the most important means of achieving improvement in the status of women would be to secure for them a fair share of employment opportunities to earmark a per centage of allocation for women and fix for them a growth target in all the poverty alleviation aprogrammes.

The long-term objective of the development programmes for women during the Sventh Five Year Plan was to raise their economic and social status in order to bring them into the mainstream of national development.

The basic approach was to inculcate confidence among women and bring about an awareness of their own potential. During the Eighth Five Year Plan, programmes designed to bring about improvement in the status of women comprised a condensed course of education for adult women and vocational training, support ot training and employment programmes for women, setting up of women's development corporations in states and the like.

Ninth Plan intends to take special measures to improve human development. For this purpose, extension of education and health care to the weaker and underprivileged sections received special priority in the Ninth Plan[28]. The underprivileged sections, includes women, scheduled castes, scheduled tribes and the like. Thirty per cent reservation for women in employment, which was announced by the Government of India recently, is considered a boon for their upliftment.

Achievements, however, expressed in terms of demographic and employment characteristics, show the position of women to be unequal. This reflects the limitations of the law to bring about substantial change. The law assumes and reinforces the conventional notions of women as having a primary responsibility to the family and motherhood and the need to preserve these roles. Majority of men are even now not quite reconciled to women's working outside home and this is considered one of the reasons for women's slow aprogress. This may be because male vanity, fed by centuries of trandition, is not ready to accept a measure of financial independence and self-assurance among women. But the old resistance to not letting women a work is being eroded by the economic imperatives of high standard of living. It has come to be realised that the working women are an asset to a middele class family without being a serious embarrassment, as long as she abides by the general decorum of the family[29].

Women strongly feel that they can capably discharge duties assigned to other kinds of jobs that are available. Majority of them further feel that they are not only capable of doing things properly but also can perform the assigned work as good as men. At any rate, it would be appreciated if they are least likely to be underestimated. They are not only confident about the performance and discharge of the assigned duties but they do want to have equal opportunities with men to prove their competence in all possible walks of life, in every profession and in all occupations[30].

The ILO Report on "women Workers in a ChangingWorld" noted that while formal discrimination in employment based on sex is tending to disappear , informal policies and practices are tending to persist. The residual forms of discrimination tend to operate formally and informally at a higher level in the occupational pyramid after blocking the advancement of women on the ground of their individual merit, irrespective of sex[31].

A study on HRD in banks shows that the banks continue to apply the same personnel policies and similar career paths for men and women. The inflexible personnel policies, often prompt women to forego promotions and continue at the clerical level. This is because, in banks,. promotions is always followed by transfer. The policies and practices of any institution should be flexible to enable the women employees to work more conveniently. The Ministry of Finance, Government of India issued gudelines to Public Sector Banks in 1986 which emphasised the policy to post hunsband and wife at the same station give, of course, the constraint of administrative feasibility. The impact of implementation of these guidelines at the bank level remains yet to be seen[32].

Their position in the labor market is not attaractive inspite of the efforts taken by the Government Machinery. While women constitute 11.19 per cent of the total human resources of nationalised banks, their distribution across differnt categories is quite uneve. Significantly enough, only 3.97 per cent of all bank officers happened to be women, while at the clerical level women constituted 17.3 per cent of the total workforce. Even at the sub-staff level, the per centage of women to total members of staff was greater than at the officer level[33].

Coverage of Women Employees in the Cooperative Sector

Women are given less opportunity not only in private and public sector organisations but their participation as employees is also less in cooperatives. Women constituted only 2.7 per cent of the total workforce of all the central cooperative banks in Tamil Nadu. Category-wise distribution shows that only 0.3 per cent of the total bank officers happended to be women while at the clerical level they constituted 3 per cent of the total work-force. The percentage of women at the sub-staff level was 2.5 which was greater than that at the officer level[34]. In other cooperatives too the same position is prevailing. Therefore, this aspect must be looked into and examined thoroughly.

In the case of urban cooperative banks, there are totally ten societies, women are found only in four. Out of the 106 employees' cooperative societies in the districts under study, only 11.3 per cent of the societies have employed women. As reagrds the consumer sector, there is cent per cent participation and 42.9 per cent of the marketing societies are having women employees. As far as the housing sector is concerned, there is a vast difference in the number of women-employed societies - 43 per cent of the total number of societies have women employees. The same condition prevails in the handloom sector where only 6.1 per cent of the total number of societies have women employees. In both the dairy cooperatives organised at district and state levels under study, women employees can be found. In state level institutions, women are employed in all the institutions except in Tamil Nadu Federation for Urban Cooperative Banks. The above data aprove that the number of societies which have employed women are a few.

The percentage of women employees are more in the cooperatives at the state level (15.4 per cent) than in the district level (9.2 per cent). In total, the percentage of women employees to total number of employees in cooperative sector in the areas selected for the study was only 11.9 per cent. The reasons for the lower share of women employees in the cooperative sector might be due to the lack of initiative taken hy the management in employing women and inadequate trained women in the field of cooeratives[35].

Conclusion

It has to be recognised that women today can no longer be regarded as the weaker sex and discriminated as second grade citizens. In order to improve their status, proper, attention is needed to eradicate illiteracy among women. It is also equally important to motivate women to work as equal partners of economic development. For assuring equality, dignity, justice, prosperity and stability, the contribution of women have to be viewed in a wider perspective.

REFERENCE

1. Poonam Sharma, "the Women-Last in, First Out," *Social Welfare,* Vol. 42, No. 5-6, Aug-Sep. 2995, p.2.
2. Hemalatha Talesse, *Higher Education among women,* New Delhi: National Publishing House, 1989, p. 6.
3. Yashodha Shanmugasundaram, *Women Employment in India,* Madras Institute for Advance Studies and Research, 1993, p. 113.
4. Lal Das. D.K., "Male Manager's Attitudes Towards Women at Work", *Indian Management,* Vol. 25, No. 1, Jan 1985, p. 18.
5. Das H., "Women Employee in Industry-A challenge to the 21st century", *Personnel Today,* Vol. XVII, No. 4, Jan Mar, 1997, p. 17.
6. Usha Talwar, *Social Profile of Working Women,* Jodhpur: Jain Brothers 1984, p. 39.
7. Deepti Bhatnagar, "HRD for Women Employees," in Anil K. Khandelwal (ed), *Human Resources Development in Banks,* New Delhi: Oxford and IBH Publishing Co. Pvt. Ltd., 1998, p. 303.
8. Deepa Mathur, *Women, Family and Work,* Jaipur: Rawat Publications, 1992 pp. 6-8.
9. Verma N.M.P. and Reshma Bano, "Discrimination of Women workers' participation: Notes on some interdisciplinary controversies," New Delhi: *Indian Journal of Industrial Relations,* Vol. 34, No. 1, July 1998, pp. 80-81.

10. Yasodha Shanmugassundaram, op. cit., p. 105.
11. Satya Sundaram.I, Women and the Economy, *Social Welfare*, Vol. 44, (5-6), Aug-Sep, 1997, p. 35.
12. Yasodha Shanmugassundaram, *op.cit.*, p. 105.
13. Naik J.P., *Status of Employment in India*, Bombay: Allied Publishers Private Limited, 1975, p. 79.
14. Editorial, *Dinakaran* (Trichy), July 8, 2000, p. 13.
15. Vimal Ranadive, "Trade Unions and Working Women", *Social Welfare*, Vol 44, No. 7. Oct. 1997, p. 27.
16. Aasha Kapur Mehta, "Liberalisation and employment of Women" in Nitya Rao, Luise Rurup, Sudharshan. Rl (eds.) *Site of Change-The structural Context for empowering women in India"*, New Delhi: Friendrich Ebert Stiftung, 1996, p. 147.
17. Agarwal K.G., "Female Executives in Government System", *Social Chage*, Vol. 20, No. 2, June 1990, p. 58.
18. Kaila H.L., "A psycho-social profile of the female exedcutive", *Social Welfare*, Vol. 46, No. 2, May 1999, p. 5.
20. *Ibid.*, p. 53.
21. *Ibid.*, p. 61.
22. Alma T. Junsay and Tim B. Heaton, *Women Working-Comparative Perspective in Developing Areas*, London: Greenwood Press Inc., 1989, pp. 2-6.
23. Deepti Bhatnagar, *op.cit.*, pp. 305-306
24. Jyotsna Rajvanshi, "Are Working Women really career conscious?", *Social Welfare*, Vol. XL (10), Jan. 1994, p. 15.
25. Deepti Bhatnagar, *op.cit.*, p. 308.
26. *Ibid.*, p. 309.
27. Pankajam Srinivasan, "Women Under Five Year Plans"—(Eds), Nancy David and Loganathan in *Women And The Economy*, Madras: Gita Press, 1993, pp. 444-458.
28. Ruddar Datt and Sundaram K.P.M., *Indian Economy*, New Delhi: S. Chand and Co Ltd., 1998, p. 874.
29. Lalitha Devi. U, *Status of Employment of Women in India*, New Delhi: B.R. Publishing Corporation, 1982, p. 17.
30. Kranti Rana, *Modern Working Women and the Development Debate*, New Delhi: Kanishka Publisher Distributors, 1998, p. 281.

31. Vidhya Rani. G, *Status of Women Employees in Government,* New Delhi: Mittal Publications, 1990, p. 45.
32. Deepti Bhatnagar, *op, cit.,* p. 310.
33. *Ibid.,* p. 304.
34. Sivaprakasam. P., *Personnel Management in central Cooperative Bank in India: Policies and Practices,* New Delhi: Kanishka Publishers, 1993, p. 46.
35. Suriakala, R., "The status of women employees in Cooperative Sector", unpubglished Ph.D. thesis, Gandhigram Rural Institute (Deemed University), 2000, pp. 18 to 19.

5

Women and Employment:

A Study of the Employment of Women in the Primary Sector in Goa

Silvia M. de Mendonca-Noronha

Introduction

Women workers constitute an important component of the Indian labour force. An increasing number of women are today compelled to leave the security of their homes and venture out in search of work. The underlying factors are numerous, depending on their socio-economic status. We can divide working women into 3 categories on a socio-economic basis.

1. Agricultural workers and those engaged in traditional menial services. This group is the largest and the poorest. Their counterparts in urban areas include, construction labour, migrant labour, domestic servants and self employed women in the informal sector.

2. The second category comparises of women who work in offices or as professionals.

3. In the third category are better educated women and those who have economic security. These

women work to ameliorate their living standards and for self-actualisation.

A majority of working women fall in the middle and lower socio-economic class and they work mainly for economic reasons. These women would have preferred to remain at home and attend to household chores and their children, than offer theselves to work. Nath (1970), found in Rajasthan, that agricultural working women of both agricultural and non-agricultural households, experessed a strong desire to be able to afford the leisure of preparing two hot meals and looking after the health and personal hygiene needs of their children, as could the high caste, higher income group of women of the area, who were not working. It was further observed that, women of the non-agricultural group, in which both men and women were workers in a cement factory, withdrew from work, as soon as the husband, or one of the sons became a paemanent worker with higher wages in the facotry. This proves that women in the lower rungs of the economic ladder work due to economic necessity.

Significance of the Study

The Primary Sector still provides employment for a large percentage of the labour force in India. Since Independence, while the composition of India's Net Domestic Product (NDP) has changed considerably, the composition of it's workforce has altered very little. The share of agriculture and allied activities in the output declined from around 52 per cent in 1951 to about 32 per cent in 1991, but their share in the workforce moved marginally from about 73 per cent to 65 per cent over the same period (Bhaduri, 1993).

We find that a large percentage of the women are employed in the agricultural sector. The main reason why we find a large percentage of women in this sector is that, as employment in other sectors demand a certain level of skill which women lack, they have no option but to fall back on agriculture for employment.

Since a large percentage of women are found in the Primary Sector, it would be interesting to know the percentage of women employed in the primary sector viz a viz that of men, if women in the primary sector are employed in 'agriculture proper' or in 'allied activities' in the primary sector, if within 'agriculture proper', they are employed as agricultural labourers or as cultivators and, if the percentage of women working as marginal workers in this sector is greater than that of men.

The paper has been divided into six sections along the following lines:

- **Section 1:** Sex Distribution of the total workforce in the Primary Sector as a whole, 1961-'91.
- **Section 2:** Sex Distribution of the worforce in 'Agriculture Proper', 1961-'91.
- **Section 3:** Sex Distribution of the workforce as, (i) Cultivators and (ii) Agricultural Labourers, 1961-'91.
- **Section 4:** Sex Distribution of the workforce in 'Activities Other than Agriculture Proper'.
- **Section 5:** Conclusion.
- **Section 6:** Policy Implications

1. Sex Distribution of the Total Workforce in the Primary Sector as a whole, 1961-'91

This section discusses the sex distribution of the total workforce in the primary sector as a whole.

From table 1 we note a decline in the workforce in the Primary Sector both in absolute terms and in percentage (refer column 7) from 1961-'91. However this decline has not been equal in male and female workers. The present section

Table 1: Sex Distribution of the Total Workforce in Goa and in the Primary Sector

Year	*Total Workforce in Goa*			*Total Workforce in the Primary Sector*		
	Males	*Females*	*Total*	*Males*	*Females*	*Total*
1	*2*	*3*	*4*	*5*	*6*	*7 (5+)*
1961	147,036	97,225	244,261	88,546 (60%)*(51%)*	83,547 (86%)	172,093 (70%)
1971	192,624	61,851	254,475	83,856 (44%)*(67%)*	41,692 (67%)*(33%)*	125,548 (49%)
1981 Main	234,975	76,272	311,247	82,230 (35%)*(67%)*	40,270 (53%)*(33%)*	122,500 (39%)
Marginal	12,367	32,595	44,962	8,974 (73%)*(24%)*	28,562 (88%)*(76%)*	37,538 (83%)
Total	247,342	108,867	356,209	91,204 (37%)*(57%)*	68,832 (63%)*(43%)*	160,038 (45%)
1991 Main	287,154	96,405	383,559	81,008 (28%)*(65%)*	42,853 (44%)*(35%)*	123,861 (32%)
Marginal	7,605	21,572	29,177	4,734 (62%)*(20%)*	18,365 (85%)*(80%)*	23,099 (79%)
Total	294,759	117,977	412,736	85,742 (29%)*(58%)*	61,218 (52%)*(42%)*	146,960 (36%)

Source: Census of India, 1961, 1971, 1981, 1991, Goa, Daman and Diu, Eocnomic Tables.

Note:
1. Figures given in brackets in columns 5 and 6 are the percentages of figures in column 2 and 3 respectively the said columns.
2. Figures given italics in 5 and 6 shows the percentage of male and female workforce in primary sector.
3. Figures given in brackets in col 7 are the percentages, of figures in column 4.

attempts to throw light on the trends in the sex distribution of the workforce in the Primary Sector during this period.

From columns 5, 6 and 7 in the table we observe the following:

1. A decline in absolute terms in the number of male workers in the Primary sector from 88,546 (col.5) in 1961 to 85, 742 in 1991.
2. The female workforce also shows a decline in absolute terms in the Primary Sector from 83,547 in 1961 to 61,218 in 1991.
3. There has been a rise in the percentage of the male workforce in the Primary Sector viz a viz that of the females, from 51% in 1961 to 58% in 1991, (refer col. 5).
4. The percentage of the female workforce in the Primary Sector in Goa viz a viz the male workforce shows a fall from 49% in 1961 to 42% in 1991, (Col.6).
5. We note a fall in the percentage of the male workforce in the Primary Sector to the male workforce in Goa from 60% in 1961 to 29% in 1991 (Col.5).
6. The percentage of the female workforce in the Primary Sector in Goa declined from 86% in 1961 to 52% in 1991, (Col. 6,).
7. Although, the percentage of the total female workforce in the Primary Sector, to the total female workforce in Goa, declined from 86% in 1961 to 52% in 1991, it was higher than the percentage of the total male workforce in the primary sector to the total male workforce in Goa, which was 60% in 1961 and declined to 29% in 1991 (refer col. 5&6).
8. The percentage of female marginal workers is higher than that of males both in 1981 and in 1991.

From the above observations we conclude the following.

1. The primary sector in Goa has been male dominated. and this domination has increased from 1961-'91.

2. More female workers out of the total female worforce in Goa (52% in 1991) are employed in the primary sector than males. This implies that the females have been getting employment mainly in the primary sector in Goa.

3. The percentage of female marginal workers in the Primary Sector is greater than that of males, which implies that more female workers are employed as marginal workers in the primary sector than males.

2. Sex Distribution of the Workforce Employed in 'Agriculture Proper', 1961-'91

This section discusses the sex distribution of the total workforce in Agriculture Proper'. 'Agriculture Proper' includes cultivators and agricultural labourers.

From the above table we make the following obervations:

1. The total male workforce in agriculture proper declined in absolute terms from 66,394 in 1961 to 58,549 in 1991.

2. We also note a decrease in absolute terms in the total female workforce in agriculture proper from 75,702 in 1961 to 54,862 in 1991.

3. The percentage of the male workforce in agriculture proper to the total male workforce in the primary sector declined from 75% in 1961 to 68% in 1991.

4. The percentage of the female workforce in agriculture proper to the total female workforce in the primary sector also declined from 91% in 1961

Table 2: Sex Distribution of the Total Workforce Employed in Agriculture Proper

Year	*Total Workforce in the Primary Sector*			*Total Workforce in Agriculture Proper*		
	Males	*Females*	*Total*	*Males*	*Females*	*Total*
1	2	3	4	5	6	7
1961	88,546	83,547	172,093	66,394 (75%)(47%)	75,702 (91%)(53%)	142,096 (83%)
1971	83,856	41,692	125,548	61,975 (74%)(63%)	36,840 (88%)(37%)	98,815 (79%)
1981	82,230	40,270	122,500	53,775 (65%)(60%)	35,157 (87%)(40%)	88,932 (73%)
Marginal	8,976	28,562	37,538	7,959 (89%)(22%)	27,552 (97%)(78%)	35,511 (95%)
Total	91,206	68,932	160,038	61,734 (98%)(49.6%)	62,709 (78%)(50.4%)	124,443 (78%)
1991	81,008	42,853	123,861	54,370 (67%)(59%)	37,442 (87%)(41%)	91,812 (74%)
Marginal	4,734	18,365	23,099	4,179 (88%)(19%)	17,420 (95%)(81%)	21,599 (94%)
Total	85,742	61,218	146,960	58,549 (68%)(52%)	54,862 (90%)(48%)	113,411 (77%)

Source: Census of India 1961, 1971, 1981, 1991, Goa, Daman and Diu, Economic Tables.

Note:
1. Percentages in italics percentages of figures in column 5 and 6 respectively with that of figures in col. 7.
2. Percentages in brackets are percentages of figures in columns 5, 6 and 7 with that of figures in cols. 2, 3 and 4 respectively.

to 90% in 1991-a marginal decline over a period of 30 years.

5. The percentage of the male workforce to the total workforce (Male+female) in agriculture proper increased from 47% in 1961 to 52% in 1991.

6. The percentage of the female workforce to the total workforce (male+female) in agriculture proper decreased from 53% in 1961 to 48% in 1991.

7. From 1981 to 1991 there has been a decline in the male marginal workers from 22% of the total workforce in agriculture proper to 19% in 1991, whereas the female workers in agriculture proper show a rise from 78% in 1961 to 81% in 1991.

From the above observations we can conclude the following:

1. Less number of male workers are being employed in agriculture proper both in absolute terms as well as in the percentage to the total workers in the primary sector from 1961-'91.

2. Most of the female workers in the primary sector are employed in agriculture proper, (90% in 1991) which implies that other avenues of employment in the primary sector are more favourable for men.

3. More females are employed as marginal workers in agriculture proper than males.

3. Sex Distribution of the Total Workforce Employed as Cultivators, 1961-'91.

This section discusses the sex distribution of the total workforce employed as cultivators from 1961-1991.

(i) Cultivators

At the outset, it is appropriate to first define the term 'cultivator' as used in the various censuses.

The 1961 Census definition: In the 1961 Census, the term 'cultivator' included both the owner cultivators, as well as tenant cultivator. Therefore, "all persons working in land, cultivation on which they had either ownership or tenancy rights were included in this category. 'Cultivation' according to this census involved ploughing, sowing and harvesting and did not include fruit growing, keeping of orchards or groves and working for plantations like coffee, tea, rubber, chinchona and other medical plantations."

The 1971 census definition: The 1971 Census says," for purposes of the census a cultivator is one who is engaged in cultivation by oneself or by supervision or direction in one's capacity as owner or leases of land held from private person (s) or institution(s) for consideration of payment in cash, kind or share. A person who merely owns land but has given out land to another person or persons for cultivation for money, kind or share of crop and who does not even supervise or direct cultivation of land, is not considered to be working as a cultivator. Similarly, a person working on another person's land for wages in cash, kind or share is also not considered as cultivator".

The 1981 Census definition: According to the definition in the 1981 Census, "a person is working as cultivator if he or she is engaged either as employer, single worker or family worker in cultivation of land owned or held from Government or held from private person or institutions for payment in money, kind or share. Cultivation includes supervision or direction of cultivation. A person who has given out his/her land to another person or persons for cultivation for money, kind or share of crop and who does not even supervise or direct cultivation of land, will not be treated as cultivator. Similarly a person working in another person's land for wages in cash or kind or a combination of both (agricultural labourer) will not be treated as cultivator."

Table 3: Sex Distribution of the Total Workforce Employed as Cultivators

Year	*Total Workforce in the Primary Sector*			*Total Workforce employed as cultivators*		
	Males	*Females*	*Total*	*Males*	*Females*	*Total*
1	*2*	*3*	*4*	*5*	*6*	*7*
1961	88,546	83,547	172,093	54,161 (61%)*(52%)*	49,978 (60%)*(48%)*	104,139 (61%)
1971	83,856	41,692	125,548	41,899 (50%)*(69%)*	18,620 (45%)*(31%)*	60,519 (48%)
1981 Main	82,230	40,270	122,500	37,321 (45%)*(64%)*	21,055 (52%)*(36%)*	58,376 (48%)
Marginal	8,976	28,562	37,538	4,236 (47%)*(22%)*	15,236 (53%)*(78%)*	19,472 (54%)
Total	91,206	68,832	160,038	41,557 (46%)*(53%)*	36,291 (53%)*(47%)*	77,848 (49%)
1991 Main	81,008	42,853	123,861	35,201 (43%)*(62%)*	21,327 (50%)*(38%)*	56,528 (46%)
Marginal	4,734	18,365	23,099	2,136 (45%)*(18%)*	9,972 (54%)*(82%)*	12,108 (52%)
Total	85,742	61,218	146,960	37,337 (44%)*(54%)*	31,299 (51%)*(46%)*	68,636 (47%)

Source: Census of India 1961, 1971, 1981, 1991, Goa, Daman and Diu, Economic Tables.

Note: (1) Percentages not underlined are percentages of figures in cols. 5 and 6 respectively with that of figures in col. 7.

(2) Underlined percentages are percentages of girures in cols. 5,6, and 7 with that of figures in cols. 2, 3, and 4 respectively.

The 1991 Census definition: According to the definition in the 1991 Census, "a person is working as cultivator if he or she is engaged either as employer, single worker or family worker in cultivation of land owned or held from Government or held from private persons or institutions for payment in money, kind or share. Cultivation includes supervision or direction of cultivation. A person who has given out his/her land to another person or persons for cultivation for money, kind or share of crop and who does not even supervise or direct cultivation of land, will not be treated as cultivator. Similarly, a person working in another person's land for wages in cash or kind or a combination of both (agricultural labourer) will not be treated as cultivator."

From Table 3 we make the following observations:

1. The number of male cultivators decreased in absolute terms from 54,161 in 1961 to 37,337 (Total figures) in 1991. The total female cultivators also declined from 49,978 in 1961 to 31, 299 in 1991.
2. The percentage of the male workforce engaged as cultivators in the primary sector declined from 61% in 1961 to 44% in 1991. The percentage of female cultivators to the total female workforce in the primary sector also declined from 60% in 1961 to 51% in 1991. However, the decline is greater in the case of male cultivators (the percentage of male cultivators declined by 17% points from 1961 to 1991 and that of female cultivators declined by 9% points).
3. We note throughout that the percentage of females engaged as cultivators has always been lower than that of males except in the case of marginal workers where we find a higher percentage of females.

From the above observations we conclude the following:

1. There seems to be a general decline in the absolute number as well as the percentage of both male and female cultivators from 1961 to 1991 in Goa.

2. More males are engaged as cultivators than females.
3. There are more female cultivators who are marginal workers than males.

(ii) Agricultural Labourers

The 1961 Census definition: According to the 1961 Census, "an agricultural labourer is one who works in another person's land only as a labourer (without exercising any supervision or direction in cultivation) for wages in cash, kind or share of produce. He should have been working as agricultural labourer in the last or in the current working season."

The 1971 Census definition: According to this Census, an agricultural labourer was, "a person who works in another person's land for wages in money, kind or share. He has no risk in the cultivation but merely works in another person's land for wages. The labourer could have no risk in the cultivation but merely works in another person's land for wages. The labourer could have no right of lease or contract on land on which he works."

The 1981 Census definition: The 1981 Census definition is the same as the 1971 Census definition. According to this Census, "a person who works on another person's land for wages in money, kind or share should be regarded as an agricultural labourer. He or she has no risk in the cultivation but he/she merely works in another person's land for wages. An agricultural labourer has no right of lease or contract on land on which he/she works."

The 1991 Census definition: According to the 1991 Census, "A person who works in another person's land for wages in money, kind or share should be regarded as an agricultural labourer. He or she has no risk in the cultivation but he/she merely works on another person's land for wages. An agricultural labourer has no right of lease or contract on land on which he/she works."

We note that the definition of agricultural labourer in the last three censuses are the same.

From the data given in Table 4 we make the following observations:

1. There was an increase in absolute number in the total male as well as female agricultural labourers from 12,233 in 1961 to 21,212 in 1991, but a decrease in the case of female agricultural labourers from 25,724 in 1961 to 23,563 in 1991.
2. The percentage of both male and female workers employed as agricultural labourers from the total male as well as female workers employed in the primary sector has increased from 1961 to 1991. In the cse of males it was from 14% in 1961 to 25% in 1991 and in the case of females it was from 31% in 1961 to 38% in 1991. The increase was greater in the case of male workers by 11% points as against 7% points in the case of females).
3. We also note from the table that from 1961 to 1991 the percentage of females engaged as agricultural labourers in greater than that of males. However from 1961 to 1991 the percentage of males employed as agricultural labourers has increased while that of females has decreased.
4. The percentage of marginal workers in the case of female agricultural labourers is greater than that of males.

From the above observations we conclude the following:

1. A higher percentage of agricultural labourers are females in Goa.

2. The percentage of females viz a viz that of males, employed as agricultural labourers is declining.
3. A high percentage of the women employed as agricultural labourers in the primary sector from 1981 to 1991 are marginal workers.

From the above table we make the following observations:

1. The total male workforce engaged in activities other than in agriculture proper increased in absolute terms from 22,152 in 1961 to 27193 in 1991, whereas there was a decline in absolute terms in the female workforce in these activities from 7,845 in 1961 to 6,356 in 1991.
2. The percentage of the total male workforce in other than agriculture proper to the total male workforce in the primary sector increased from 1961 to 1991 by 7% points, i.e. from 25% in 1961 to 32% in 1991, whereas the percentage of the total female workforce in other than agriculture proper to the total female workforce in the primary sector increased only marginally by 1% point from 9% in 1961 to 10% in 1991.
3. From 1961 to 1991 we note that the percentage of the male workforce engaged in other than agriculture proper was much higher than that of the female workers (refer percentages that given italics in cols. 5 and 6).

From the above observations we conclude that this sector is more conducive to the employment of men rather than women.

From the analysis of the above tables we conclude the following.

Table 4: Sex Distribution of the Total Workforce Employed as Agricultural Labourers

Year	*Total Workforce in the Primary Sector*			*Total Agricultural Labourers*		
	Males	*Females*	*Total*	*Males*	*Females*	*Total*
1	2	3	4	5	6	7
1961	88,546	83,547	172,093	12,233 (14%)*(32%)*	25,724 (31%)*(68%)*	37,957 (22%)
1971	83,856	41,692	125,548	20,076 (24%)*(52%)*	18,220 (44%)*(48%)*	38,296 (31%)
1981 Main	82,230	40,270	122,500	16,454 (20%)*(54%)*	14,102 (35%)*(46%)*	30,556 (25%)
Marginal	8,976	28,562	37,538	3,723 (23%)	12,316 (77%)	16,039 (43%)
Total	91,206	68,832	160,038	20,177 (22%)*(43%)*	26,418 (38%)*(57%)*	46,595 (29%)
1991 Main	81,008	42,853	123,861	19,169 (24%)*(54%)*	16,115 (38%)*(46%)*	35,284 (28%)
Marginal	4,734	18,365	23,099	2,043 (43%)*(22%)*	7,448 (41%)*(78%)*	9,491 (41%)
Total	85,742	61,218	146,960	21,212 (25%)*(47%)*	23,563 (38%)*(53%)*	44,775 (30%)

Source: Census of India 1961, 1971, 1981, 1991, Goa, Daman and Diu, Economic Tables.

Note:
1. Percentages in italics are percentages of figures in Cols. 5 and 6 with that of figures in col. 7 respectively.
2. Percentages given in brackets are percentages of figures in cols. 5, 6 and 7 with that of figures in cols. 2, 3 and 4 respectively.

5. Conclusion

1. More female workers are engaged in the primary sector than males.
2. compared to males there are more female marginal workers in the primary sector.
3. As compared to males, more females in the primary sector are engaged in agriculture proper which implies that, the other areas in the primary sector were more favourable for men.
4. Female marginal workers form 81% of the total marginal workers in agriculture in 1991. From 1981-'91, there has been in increase in the percentage of female marginal workers in agriculture proper from 78% in 1981 to 81% in 1991.
5. In agriculture proper, a higher percentage of women workers are employed as agricultural labourers than as cultivators from 1961 to 1991, whereas more males are employed as cultivators.
6. More males are employed in "other than agriculture proper" than females, indicating that activities outside agriculture proper are more favourable for the employment of male workers.

Thus we conclude that in the primary sector, women are by and large employed in Agriculture Proper. Within this category they are largely employed as agricultureal labourers, and that too a large percentage of them work as marginal labourers.

6. Policy Implications

From the above study, we find that the percentage of women employed in the primary sector is higher than that of men. Within the primary sector, women are largely employed as agricultural labourers and a much higher

Table 5: Sex Distribution of the Total Work Force Employed in Activities other than Agriculture Proper

Year	*Total Workforce in the Primary Sector*			*Total Workforce in other than Agriculture proper*		
	Males	*Females*	*Total*	*Males*	*Females*	*Total*
1	*2*	*3*	*4*	*5*	*6*	*7*
1961	88,546	83,547	172,093	22,152 (25%)*(74%)*	7,845 (9%)*(26%)*	29,997 (17%)
1971	83,856	41,692	125,548	21,881 (26%)*(82%)*	4,852 (12%)*(18%)*	26,733 (21%)
1981 Main	82,230	40,270	122,500	28,455 (35%)*(85%)*	5,113 (13%)*(15%)*	33,568 (27%)
Marginal	8,976	28,562	37,538	1,017 (11%)*(50.2%)*	1,010 (3.5%)*(49.8%)*	2,027 (5%)
Total	91,206	68,832	160,038	29,472 (32%)*(83%)*	6,123 (9%)*(17%)*	35,595 (22%)
1991 Main	81,008	42,853	123,861	26,636 (33%)*(83%)*	5,411 (13%)*(17%)*	32,049 (26%)
Marginal	4,734	18,365	23,099	555 (12%)*(37%)*	945 (5%)*(63%)*	1500 (6%)
Total	85,742	61,218	146,960	27,193 (32%)*(81%)*	6,356 (10%)*(19%)*	33,549 (23%)

Source: Census of India, 1961, 1971, 1981, 1991, Goa, Daman and Diu, Economic Tables.

Note:
1. Percentages in italics are percentages of figures in cols., 5,6 and 7 with that of figures in cols. 2, 3 and 4 respectively.
2. Percentages given in brackets are percentages of figures in cols. 5 and 6 with that of figures in col.7.

percentage of women are employed as marginal workers than men.

The primary sector being an unorganised sector, it increases the opportunities to exploit women. Therefore, the government should take extra precaution to protect the rights of women, who are easy targets for exploitation by their employers, by appropriate legislations to safeguard their interests. These legislations should be constantly monitored, to make sure that they are properly implemented.

Within the primary sector, more employment opportunities should be created in allied activities for women, as it is found that in this sub-sector, the percentage of women employed is very low. This will enable women to earn higher incomes. This will also enable them to be gainfully employed. These allied activities could be home-based, which will enable more women to take up such activities with ease. Training programmes can be started for women in animal husbandry, rural crafts etc. However these training programmes, should be so designed, as to take account of the dual roles women play as producers and family nurturers. Training should not involve long absences from home, with the onset of economic reforms in India, and the increasing importance given to informal sector activities, women can find themselves gainfully employed in such activities.

The government should seriously implement the various schemes for self employment of women in rural areas such as DWCRA (Development of Women and Children in Rural Areas), IRDP (Integrated Rural Development Programme) etc.

REFERENCES

Anker R., Buvinic M. and Youssef N.H., (1982) *Women's Role and Population Trends in the Third World*, Croom Helm, London.

Anker R., (1983), "Female Labour Participation in Developing Countries", *International Labour Review* Vol. 122, No. 6.

Banerjee, N., (1999), "Women in the Emerging Labour Market", *The Indian Journal of Labour Economics*, Vol. 42, No. 4.

Bhaduri, A. (1993), *"Structural Adjustment, Labour Market and Employment in India"*, ILO-ARTEP.

Director of Census Operations, Goa, Daman and Diu, *"Census of India, 1961, Goa, Daman and Diu, Economic Table."*

——, Goa, Daman and Diu, *"Census of India, 1971, Goa, Daman and Diu, Economic Tables."*

——, Goa, Daman and Diu, *"Census of India, 1981, Goa, Daman and Diu, Economic Tables."*

——, Goa, *"Census of India, 1991, Goa, Economic Tables"*.

6

Role of Women in the Self-help Group:

An Emerging Possibility of Cooperativisation at Grass Root

Ranjit Karmakar & Bholanath Ghosh

Self sufficiency, self-help and co-operations are very much interlinked words in social science literatures. Process of co-operation in human society is universal and to form society human interaction needs to be co-operated in times of exigences and in many occasion which are of social nature.

There have been many experiments with the rural developments in India since independence and even evidences are there in pre-independence era too, to develop the countryside. In 1904 Government of British India enacted laws to form co-ops. in order to free the farmers from the clutches of rural money lender operating in the rural India.

Co-operatives as formal organisations for doing business by peoples of small means have been acknowledged by government on recommendations of experts and policy makers. Researchers, concern for improving the economic means of smaller people has been referred in their work time and again. As a result, there were efforts from different rural development organisations in different times both on the part of the Government and non-government organisations.

Our study is concerned with such an attempt organised in a limited scale in village situations in Mindnapore district. This effort has been done mainly by women forming a self-help group to help themselves in time of needs and emergency. We see this effort as an exercise towards co-operativisation process. The possibilities may in the long run take the shape of a co-operative venture. As such, our discussion will be on a self-help group's possibility of transforming as co-operative and impact on the social and economic its of the life of sphere women. Hence, we discuss the co-operative these elements in the formation of these self help groups (SHGs).

In this regard, we can examine some of the definitions of co-operatives in order to view the presence of elements of co-operatives in the formation of such self-help groups of women.

Co-operatives are viewed as an appendage of not only rural developments but have they been given due weightage in urban co-operation as well.

Here we quite some of the definitions of co-operations and co-operatives clear to its efficacy in area of SHGs. There are many definitions of co-operations and accordingly many attributes have been attached with the idea by many authors.

According to C.F. Strickland, "Every group of individuals, associated to secure a common end and by joint effort, may be said to co-operate, for instance, a football team, a gang of robbers or the share holders of speculative company. A century of history has given co-operation with a capital "C" a more precise meaning; it indicates the associations of individuals to secure common economic and by honest means; it is also essential in many forms of co-operations that the individuals possess a personal knowledge of one another."[1]

1. C.F. Strickland, Co-operation in India, p. 15)

Seligman defines co-operation as such "Co-operation in its technical sense means the abandonment of competition in distribution and production and the elimination of the middleman of all kinds."[2]

The Maclegan Committee on Co-operation defines co-operation in these words: "The theory of co-operation is very briefly, that an isolated and powerless man can, by association with other and by moral development and mutual support obtain in his own degree the material advantage available to weather and powerful persons and thereby develop himself to the fullest extent of his natural abilities."....

According to the Co-operative Planning Committee (1946). "Co-operation is a form of organisation in which persons voluntarily associate together on a basis of equality for the promotion of their economic interests. Those who come together have a common economic aim which they cannot achieve by individual isolated action because of the weakness of the economic position of a large majority of them. This element of individual weakness is overcome by the pooling of their resources, by making self-help effective through mutual aid and by strengthening the bonds of moral solidarity between them."

James Peter Warbase observes that "Co-operation is a way of life thereby people unite democratically in the sprit of mutual aid to get the largest possible access to the things and services they need."[3]

So, from the above definition of co-opeation, we can state briefly that co-operatidve society is a voluntary organisation of human beings where the members exercise equal rights and have equal voice, in a spirit of self-help and

2. Seligman, Principles of Economies. p. 151.)
3. Manes P. Warbasse. The Co-operative Way (New York, 1946).

mutual help and share its fruits in proportion to the contribution which each has made towards its business.

Hence, the principles on which the co-operative activities are based may be laid down as follows:

(a) A voluntary association.

(b) Democratic organisation.

(c) Self-help through mutual help.

(d) Common welfare.

(e) A spirit of Service.

It has been argued that a co-operative society, if organised, on the basis of above principles and on this line will inevitably strengthen the weaker sections through the economic benefit and social and moral upliftment. It has also been thought that in an acute competitive market economy, the rural producers can take part in the market by organising their labour and capital and their product on the co-operative line so that they might overcome in the competition with strong big entrepreneurs. Thus co-operative of the small rural producers and big private trading organisations of industry can co-exists in even competitive market economy. Though theoretically it sounds good and co-operative is the only alternative for small rural producers but what our experience tells?

Co-operative movement has been succeeded in many spheres in the west as we find documented well in various reports and co-operative journals. But what is story of success and failure in Indian co-operatives which are supposed to be the egalitarian agents in the society? It is of great question.

There are various types of co-operatives all over the globe. But primacy of production based co-operatives are more pronounced than store-based co-operatives. The forces of market economy can be better challenged by forming working men's co-operatives. It has been emphasized by even Karl Marx that in fighting the market forces, struggles of the working class has a greater role to play in overthrowing or blunting the process of market forces. The workers' co-operative is one of the weapons which can challenge the supremacy of the capitalists over the means of production. Organising consumers' co-operatives is a less effective means because they adapt to the present system, rather than challenge it. He therefore states : "We recommend to the working men to embark on co-operative production rather than the co-operative stores. The latter touch the surface of the present economic system, the former attacks its ground work".[4]

Marx also recommended that workers' co-operatives must try to promote similar endeavour by spreading the movement to other industries and through propagation of its principles: "We recommend to all co-operative society to connect one part of their joint income into a fund for propagating their principles by example as well as by precept, in other words, by promoting the establishment of new co-operative fabrics, as well as by teaching and preaching".[5]

It may be noted that of the nine points recommended by Marx to the First Congress of the International Working Men's Association, six were adopted, which included the one on co-operative Labour.[6] In 1868, at its Brassels Congress, the International Working Men's Association emphasized the role of trade unions in promoting workers' co-operatives. In fact in its resolution on 15th September. 1868, it recommended that the ultimate objectives of trade unions should be to transform themselves into workers companies : "If we are such partisans of trade unions, it is not only with

4. K. Marx and F Engles, Selected works, volume-2, Progress Publishers, Moscow, 1976, pp. 81-82.
5. *Ibid.*, p. 82.)
6. *Ibid.*, p. 441, note No. 38.

regard to the necessities of the present, but also the future social order. To explain, we do not simply consider these as necessary palliatives, (note that we do not say remedies), no our views are much higher. From the bottom of the chaos and misery in which we struggle, we lift our eyes to a more harmonious and happly society. Then we see in these trade unions, the embryos of the great workers' companies which will one day replace the Capitalist Companies with their thousands of wage- earner, at least in all industries whose collective force is used and there is no middle way between wage slavery and association. (As has been shown by recent strikes, Union funds may be used for setting up co-operative productive societies)."

So from the discussion so far, two important aspects emerge. Firstly, the constructive role of workers' co-operatives in training and building confidence among the working class in their struggle for controlling the means of production. Secondly, the role of trade unions in promoting these institutions. It is implied that in order that trade unions play a significant role in the class struggle their efforts must be beyond the realm of challenging the capitalist system merely through wage struggles. Apart from organising workers to unitedly fight for better living and working conditions (which, no doubt, is an important aspect of class struggle) the trade union movement must practically demonstrate to the working class that they are capable of controlling the means of production.

Another very important aspect of workers' co-operative centres around the role of the State. Marx has been very categorical in excluding interference or initiative of the State in formation and management of these institutions. In 1875, he launched a broadside against the idea of establishing producers' co-operatives with State aid, as proposed in the draft programmes of the United Workers' Party of Germany (also known as the Gotha Programme). When toiling people demand State aid to set-up Co-operatives it only expresses "its full Consciousness, that it neither rules nor is ripe for ruling."[7]

If co-operatives are to be used as tools of the workers in their class struggle they must emerge from the genuine desire of the worker to control the means of production and emancipate themselves from the shackles of capitalism. They have to draw their strength from their own class and not from any external agency like State or the Government. The following extract from the Critique of the Gotha Programmes might be put here be in this regard.

"That the workers desire to establish the conditions for co-operatives production on a social scale, and first of all on a national scale, in their own country, only means that they are working to revolutionise the present conditions of production, and it has nothing in common with the foundation of co-operative societies with State aid. But as far as present co-operative societies are concerned, they are of value only in so far as they are the independent creations of the workers and not the proteges either of governments or of the bourgeios."[8]

So from the discussion above, co-operative's efficiency has been useful for a radical change in production relations as well to bring about a new mode of productions in the society. None can deny the importance of a system based on co-operation rather than based on monetary system. But how far this is possible particularly in India where studies on co-operatives have not been popular in both Government and among the researchers as well. There are risks in taking up studies on co-operatives. People at the State will raise their

7. K. Marx, Critique of the Gotha Programmes, Progress Publishers, Moscow, 1976, p. 24.
8. *Ibid.*, p. 24.

eyebrow at studying the co-operation particularly the workers' co-op. whose ambition is great.

One can also take the risk of the onslaught of state power and die even at starvation when taking up co-operatives as subject matter of his study. Because, people generally are individualistic by nature. He wants the gratification of his /her self as the foremost. Then becomes social. To revert this situation is a Herculean task and anyone to do this will endanger himself and his initiatives will be frown upon This is quite another thing. Obviously, there are people who despite this hardship will take on this path.

Initiative by Women to Form Co-operatives

Now we can see, the rudimentary co-operation has given birth of self-help group of women who by dire need of existence, has come to form groups to help themselves. Of course, we can see that some of the principles of co-operations are at work in the formation of self-help Group of Women. The name 'self-help group' itself directly signifies that it is a voluntary organisation of women and the spirit is based on Self-help and distribution is according to the need. So some of the principles of Co-operation are applicable in case of the self-help group formation by some women in Medinipur district. It has no relation with the production system or state help. Rather it is emerged from the need to come together and in times of exigency, it even sanctions loans to its members.

It may be said that SHGs of women are in footing to be against the odds of times. However, we can examine the SHGs role in the light of their impact upon the members and to bring about the social change it expects to bring about. Some of the features of the Co-operation such as (i) voluntariness in association, (ii) spirit of self-help, (iii) common welfare, and (iv) spirit of service, all these four features of co-operatives are present in the SHGs under study. But we can not say that democratic norms are not followed while conducting meetings of the SHGs.

Hence, we can state that though the SHGs are not on production or consumers based but it is an association of women (persons) who have come to aid themselves during the emergency of their odds. Then one can raise the question as to why we attempt on co-operation, which is basically a formal organisation. We can say that the very basis of SHGs is the co-operation among some individuals who are women. Unlike business organisations it is a group which has a common end to benefit themselves and a mutual way of understanding among them.

So we find that mutuality, elements of self-help and spirits of service are most notable features among the SHGs. Our discussion also proceeds that it is not co-operatives in a formal way but rather it has emerged out of informal co-operation at the time of specific needs. Hence, it differs from business co-operatives with specific set of democratic functioning. The differences, underlies here as it has no specific aim of altering any production relation rather it has an adaptive character to the system's demand and economic needs the fulfillment of. In that light we shall see in later discussion the SHGs role in rendering service to its members.

Also we shall try to focus on its impact on the rural development programmes in relation to the economic development and social development of the members and others who may not directly associated with the organisation.

Our study of SHGs centres on one village in Medinipore district and they do not form any institutional agency. Rather apparent ends of them are to render both economic services and its influence on some indirect social habit generating organisations.

The self-help Group (SHG) is a viable alternative to achieve the objectives of rural development and to get community participation in all rural development programmes. Its aim is to disburse micro credit to the rural women for the purpose of making them enterprising also and encouraging them to enter into entrepreneurial activities. Credit needs of the rural women can be fulfilled totally through the SHG. The SHGs led by women have successfully demonstrated how the mobilisation and management of thrift, apprise credit needs, maintain linkages with the banks and enforce financial self discipline.

The Self-Help-Group has members not exceeding 20 and each group select among its members a leader called animator. The animators conduct one meeting every week either in morning or evening time depending on the leisure time of the group members. The group members save regular amount of Rs. 10 to Rs. 20 every week. If one is unable to save Rs. 10, she may save Rs. 5 also. The group rotates the money to the needy members for various purposes at a specified interest rate. As the repayment is per ascendant the recycling is very fast, the savings amount increases faster owing to the accumulation of income from interest. Saving habit paves the way for the empowerment of women and builds up confidence in them that they could stand on their own feet. After the group established over a period of 12 months or more in the management of its own funds, it conducts regular meetings, maintain savings and give loans to members on interest.

The self-help groups are being linked with the banks for the external credit under the projects of rural development. The joint appraisal teams consisting of bank managers, rural development officers, NGOs, project implementation units visit the groups and select the beneficiaries proposed by the women groups for providing financial assistance to the respective entrepreneurial activities. Banks provide financial assistance for various entrepreneurial activities such as setting up of petty shops, vegetable shops, tailoring units, charcoal making units, dairying etc. (The Hindu, 1st November, 1990).

Self Help Groups enhance the equality of status of women as participants, decision-makers and beneficiaries in the democratic, economic, social and cultural spheres of life. In all stages of economic and social activities, involvement of women becomes essential. They encourage women to take active part in the socio-economic progress of our nation. Mahatma Gandhi, father of our nation has stated that "women are the noblest of God's creation, supreme in their own sphere of activity." The SHGs bring out the supremacy of women in moulding the community in right perspective and explore the initiative of women in taking up entrepreneurial ventures. Women's contribution to national development is crucial. The process of economic development would be incomplete unless women are fully involved in it.

A BRIEF DESCRIPTION OF THE SHGS IN SANKRAIL BLOCK, MEDINIPUR DISTRICT, WEST BENGAL

All together 20 self-help groups have emerged in the Sankrail area of the Medinipur district. They have been operating in that area since one year or so. The experiment on SHGs is going well in the area. Each SHG comprises 10-20 members. So all together 400, in largest possibility may be the members of SHGs under discussion. Important of this is that the women meet together for the SHGs meetings and at the same time they gain some knowledge of different problems and the village and their development also.

By doing so, the women learn to work in a group and help them in times of need. Also they act as agents of social change in the area of operation and its adjacent area as well.

Group cohesiveness is another factor which is very much needed to form their organisation. The second function is the economic function which is primarily aimed to propagate among them habit of savings in order to take loan for productive purpose.

In the next discussion, we see how the self-help groups can have a definite impact at village level in different aspects of rural life.

Feedback from SHGs

We have here some feedback of SHGs from Sankrail block of Medinipore district. Data from18 self-help groups with 287 members shows that they have saved by the end of one year Rs. 23,245.00. The women met 204 times in different meetings so far. This is not a negligible performance by the women in one block of Medinipur district. The amount of savings is not important here. Important is the group habit and group itself takes the responsibility of disbursing the loan and as the loan is given for productive purpose, there is less possibility of wastage of money.

Loan Disbursed and Loan Repaid

So far 14 SHGs have sanctioned loan amounting to Rs. 24850.00 in 10 SHGs., Rs. 7700.00 has been repaid within one year period. The loan which was disbursed among 124 applicants. There was differential amount of loan disbursed in favour of different individuals. As the data does not give any caste/community background of the loanee families, we cannot say who they are by castes. That is not necessary at all for our purpose.

But we can say some women formed groups to save themselves and trying to mobilise their resources on their own and for their own upliftment. Quite naturally, this is very much encouraging and enlightening to us.

Some Performance of the SHGs

Loan distributed and loan repaid can be a criteria to judge the performance in monetary terms. Though one can argue that loan distributed and loan recovery cannot be the only function of rural based organisation run by women aiming at social performance. Despite all this arguments, we give here some data on loan recovery and loan distribution which may at least give some ideas about the position of SHGs and their potentialities.

Table 1: Disbursement of Loan in Self-help Groups in Sankrail Block, Medinipur District

SHGs	*Loan given (%)*	*Loan repaid(%)*
1	128.32	43.29
2	86.02	0.0
3	00.00	0.0
4	80.88	7.35
5.	0.0	0.0
6	69.76	9.09
7	62.89	0.00
8	89.17	0.00
9	0.00	0.00
10	148.18	33.89
11	130.95	52.27
12	90.02	32.14
13	146.75	35.29
14	82.04	33.33
15	148.18	33.33
16	139.83	00.00
17	00.00	00.00
18	00.00	00.00

The loan recovery position has exceeded in one SHG. The rate of recovery is more than 50%. The overall rate of recovery amongst all the 18 SHGs varied between 43.29% to 7.35%. In 5 cases of SHGs loan repayment has been 33.33% to 35.29%.

Conclusion

Self-help groups enhanced the status of women as participants, decision-makers and beneficiaries in the democratic, economic and socio-cultural life. In all stages of economic and social activities, involvement of women becomes essential. They encourage women to take active part in the socio-economic progress of the nation.

The emancipation of women is an essential pre-requisite for economic development and social progress of the nation. The SHGs empower women The SHGs inculcated a level of have confidence in the minds of rural women to succeed in their day to day life.

Therefore, the concept of SHGs preaches "Self-help though mutual help for common good." It is an ideal combination of one's rights and responsibilities.

REFERENCES

Gurumoorthy, T.R., self-help Groups-Empower Rural Women; in Kurukshetra; August, 2000, pp. 10-15.

Nagayya, D., Micro-Finance for Self-Help Group; Kurukshetra; August, 2000.

Marx, K. and Engles, F., Selected works, Volume 2, Progress Publishers, Moscow, 1979.

Sen, Amartaya: Gender and Co-operative Conflicts; ITOOk (ed.)—Persistence Inequalities, Helsinki, WIDER; 1987.

Acknowledgement

We express our gratitude to Dr. Nandini Das Gupta, Director of Rural Development Association and Sri Binay Kumar Mahato, who work in the same organisation for their co-operation extended to us.

7

Modernisation, Development and Gender Issues

Dr. Sushila Jain

Introduction

During the past few decades the concept of modernisation and development has covered a vast majority of literature throughout the academic world the seemingly impact of it has not only blurred our eyes but also our minds. Therefore, what is good in the interest of the society and individual, there is no time to see, think and feel about it. This is a new dilemma in the history of mankind which has been created by man himself in the course of its own development process leading to degeneration of human values.

This situation is bad and needs to be changed. But what could be the basis of this change? Its basic value structure is as important as the question of change itself. Development is not merely economic development. To think of development merely in terms of gross national production and gross national income is erroneous. Development devoid of resource generation for employment is a European concept which is surprisingly a matter of great tension and anxiety. The dysfunctional consequences of liberalisation and globalisation are evident in many developing countries and its indicators are available in India too. Therefore, the need is to understand economic development along with social, cultural, psychological and moral dimensions of development. In other words development has to be given a human base because until and unless we understand poverty and its related problems in a sensitive manner there is no sense of democracy or development.

In the process therefore, redistribution of resources naturally becomes a part and parcel of growth. Three important elements in development are (i) livelihood (ii) self dignity (iii) and freedom of selection of choices.

Rethinking about modernisation three characteristics may be identified.

1. It is a painstaking process. Because development and modernisation are based on the exploitation and indifference of a large group of people. Colonial expansion has helped a lot in this direction. It has given rise to differences at the national as well international levels. This aspect of hurting through the process of development and modernisation has been upheld correct as part of the indispensable process, not by those who have been hurt but by those who have been trying to hurt. Now this process is being challenged openly.

2. Modernisation and development are multilinear and multivariate processes.

3. These processes may not be accepted as continuous and endless processes. As they are bound by internal and external limitations. The perspective and understanding may also change. The path and goals of modernisation and development are already in a process of change.

Therefore, to think over the success of the process of modernisation is painful and to think of its future consequences is frightening. Because of the dichotomies involved in this process.

As we have reached into the 21st century the future in terms of environmental problems etc. reminds us of the disastrous aspects of environmental degradation problems. On the whole it reminds us that man has not been wise in its developmental programmes as he feels helpless in solving environmental problems and the vices of the system such as economic inflation, growing unemployment etc. The logical challenge to this process has been presented by women's freedom movements, which has shown that women is not treated as an individual but as a fractured (segmental) personality (i.e. treated as an object of sex). Devaluation of moral values is not looked down upon, corruption has become a way of life. If these are the essential pre-equisites of modernisation than Gandhian model of limited use of machines and technology and listening to the inner voice of the individual would be an appropriate solution for vices of modern civilisation and would be an appropriate path of development in India. Otherwise development and modernisation will breakdown and tradition would reestablish itself. Education and means of communication have to be effectively greared up for better expression of change in the value system. For structural changes, public opinion and purposeful administrative endeavour is required. Development and modernisation at this stage have become synonymous to each other as both have limited the distance between production and profit distribution dimensions.

The Politics of Survival

Development has to give way to sustainable development and growth has to give way to green growth. In this context a few questions have been raised by Vandana Shiva which are as follows:

1 The very question or the misconception that third world countries need development and can not afford the luxry of protecting natures ecological processes.

2. Poor people can not be a source of ecological solutions, they are merely a source of environmental problems.

3. Development is not universally benign.

4. Development for some means underdevelopment and dispossession of many.

5. Development interventions aimed at commercialisation of natural resources involves a major shift in the manner in which right to resources are perceived and exercised. It transforms commons into commodities and deprives the politically weak communities of access to resources and robs resources from nature, to generate growth on the market for more privileged groups in society.

6. This transformation in the third word countries is often state mediated though the final outcome is privatisation.

7. Most critical ecology movements are based on the need to protect nature and the need to strengthen peoples collective rights to common resources.

8. Multilateral development agencies give loans to environmentally sensitive economy and the survival economy as dispensable.

9. The third world embodics both methaphorically and symbolically Third system based neither on the supremacy of the state nor the market but on the supremacy of the citizen.

10. Third world ecology movements which resist the destruction caused by state managed market development are challenging the concepts of politics and economics as defined within the narrow confines of the market. They reveal that there is a notion of democracy which is wider and deeper than market democracy based on the recognition of the right to life of non human nature and all segments of human society, including large numbers which do not and cannot produce and consume within the market and who are treated as dispensable in the logic of the market. They also show that there is a wider concept of economy which is based on the maintenance of life and livelihood, not merely on the accumulation of profits.
11. Therefore, in an era of green capitalism where justice has become obsolete and has been separated from issues of sustainability. Peoples ecology movement highlight the way into which issues of ecology, equity, sustainability and justice are intimately linked to one another.

Gender Issues

The rise of gender sensibility is one of the distinguishing features of our times for all practical purposes, the concern for gender equity has graduated to the level of a policy objective. More importantly, it has begun to dominate public discourse over-shadowing vital concerns for other kinds of inequalities such as caste and classes. (Sharma 2000).

Two perspectives have emerged in the contemporary discourse on the modalities of gender equity. Women's development and women's empowerment. It is Ester Boserup's pioneering work women's role in Economic development (1970) which paved way to the rise of women's development perspective. The development strategy, however, has come under severe interrogation not only for its failure to deliver its promise but also for working against the interests of woman kind. Consequently, the decade of 90's has witnessed the rise of women's empowerment perspective which shot into prominence at Beijing conference. Lately, skeptical notes have begun to appear about the soundness of women's empowerment perspective, necessitating its dispassionate appraisal. The main argument advanced by S.L. Sharma is that in its present form, it betrays a pronounced western ethnocentric bias, places too heavy a reliance on conscientisation as the key strategy of women's empowerment, and above all, is marked by a measure of antagonism against man. For the same reason, it is not likely to go too far towards achieving the objective of gender equality. Hence, the need to rethink it.

Need for Women's Development Perspective

While women represent 50 percent of the world population, they perform two thirds of all working hours, receive one-tenth of the world income and own less than one percent of world property. (Humphery Institute of Public affairs). Such is the scale of 'gender gaps' in the distribution of work resources and benefits.

To tackle the problems of gender inequalities, there emerged the strategy of women's development. But the available evidences indicate that the development strategy followed so far has mostly by passed women it has actually served to reinforce the existing gender inequalities. Boserup has attributed it to planners's failure to understand the nature of gender inequalities or their unconscious gender prejudices. Critical of Boserup's explanation, a number of other scholars including Studadt. (1982), Bandarage (1984) and Maguire (1984) have explained it in terms of the inherently asymmetrical nature of development itself. They contend that the prevailing model of development is both capitalistic and patriarchal which is why it is exploitative of everything faminine, including nature and women alike.

The fact remains that women have not received a fair deal from development endeavour. It is this realisation that led Boserup as well as many others to construct a strong case for devising a gender sensitive strategy of development and a gender responsive index of development. The whole thrust was on treating women as partners in development rather than as mere beneficiaries of it. The plea was for the recognition of women's economic agency in development i.e. her productive role over and above her reproductive role. No wonder that it served as "the fundamental text for the U.N. Decade for women" (Tinker, 1990). Caroline Moser has pleaded for 'gender planning' (1989) and devising a gender development index and happily, the UN has adopted her suggestion regarding gender development index and has devised one that has become a standardised measure of gender development. Thus women in development (WID) and gender and development (GAD) are the two phases of Women's development perspective appeared with the Molyneux's work Mobilisation without emancipation (985). A major critique of women's development perspective appeared with this. Molyneux makes a seminal distinction between women's practical needs and 'strategic interests'. Women's practical needs are related to their biological make up, their conditions of living, their work loads, roles and responsibilities, these include the need for provision of maternity and child care centres, nearby water supply, stove for efficient cooking, training in sewing and weaving, etc. Strategic interests, on the other hand, arise from the mechanisms of women's subordination to men, the given gender power structure and the search for strategies to dismantle them. The socialist feminists have critiqued women's development perspective for its pre occupation with women's practical needs' to the neglect of their 'strategic interests.'

Another important critique of women's development perspective pointed to its neglect of power dimension; her say in the decision making process, her participation in domestic as well as community power structure. Stimulated by Molyneux's idea of 'strategic interests' Sara Longwe developed an analytical framework for 'gender awareness' which paved the way to women's empowerment perspective.

Women's Empowerment Perspective

Women's empowerment signifies increase in women's power to achieve equality with men. The Harvard framework for women's empowerment entails five levels of gender equality [based on Sara Longwe's formulation (1991) Material Welfare, access to resources and benefits, conscientization (debunking the belief in the natural determination of gender inequality), participation in decision making process, and above all, control over one's life and levers of power. Welfare for example, signifies the social dimension of empowerment, access to opportunities and resources the economic dimension and participation and control the political dimension, Empowerment is about social transformation , it is about radical social and it is about the people-ordinary-common. The term empowerment presupposes primacy of power over other dimensions. Griffen defines women's empowerment as adding to women's power' (1989), Kabeer interprets it as a radical transformation of power relations between women and men. So that women have greater power over their own lives and men have less power over women's lives' (1990: 8) A, Beteille observes . . . . the main point behind empowerment is that it seeks to change society through a rearrangement of power, Giddens views it as 'transformative capacity' (1984), Viewing power itself as genedered, some feminists have sought to define empowerment as 'power to' unlike men who define it as 'power over' (Deutchman 1991). The most important point in this framework is that conscientization holds the key to women's empowerment i.e. acquisition of critical awareness about the structure of discrimination, exploitation and oppression in which one is placed. It also involves organisation and mobilisation of women to attain the end of gender equality. Clearly, women's empowerment is different from women's development-perspective Women's development is primarily a socio-economic project, while women's empowerment according to some scholars is essentially a political project. Analytically separable, the two are, however, empirically interrelated.

Towards Social Rearrangement

Recently the French structuralists have argued that the social structure draws heavily from linguistic structure. For these theorists, language is symbolic. Language is power and therefore when we say that there is empowerment of women we want to stress that women have power of knowledge.

In this context we would refer to Michel Foucault (1976) who says that power is nothing but knowledge. In other words those who have power have knowledge. On the basis of such an understanding of power and empowerment, we would refer to some propositions which emerged from the writings of Foucault.

1. Power is not something that is acquired, seized or shared, something that one holds on to or allows to slip away; power is exercised from innumerable points.

2. Relations of power are found in economic processes, knowledge relationships and sexual relations.

3. Power comes from below : that is, there is no binary and all encompassing opposition between rulers and ruled at the root of power relations. One must suppose that manifold relationships of force that take shape and come into play in the machinery of products in families, limited groups and institutions.

4. Power relations are both intentional and non-subjective.

Foucault had argued that the sources of power were many. It means that power is not derived only from constitutional amendment. This is only one known source of power, but this source is a multiplier. It opens up new sources of power, normally, family, caste, religion, village etc. In the second proposition, which assumes importance in the context of Indian society, Foucault argued that power relations are not only in terms of ruler and ruled, the dominant and the subordinate. It is in fact a network of social relations. Power is found in economy, knowledge and sex. Yet another implication of power proposition as given by Focault is that power is derived from below. It involves manifold relations of force. It involves the whole process of production and consumption. It is found in groups and institutions.

Foucault has given new dimension to power analysis. Such an analysis has wider implications in India. Andre Betcille argues that empowerment in Indian context has become very comprehensive. His observations run as :

The most radical theories of empowerment are those that called for the empowerment of the people as a whole. These are populist theories and they are mistrustful of institutions as such, because they seen them as obstacles to the aspirations of the ordinary people-peasants, workers, students, dalits, women to secure control over their own lives. They ignore or reject the distinction that social theories have been at pains to make, between marked power and legitimate authority. They believe that the well being of institutions is best secured by having full and equal participation by all in the conduct of their affairs; for the historically minded, the model of such institution is the Pairs Commune of eighteenth century, once greatly admired by Marx.

Deconstrction of Patriarchy

Recently, post Modernity has stressed for a new theory in social sciences. The post modern theorists, such as Habarmas, Bourdeau and Derrida have opined that the traditional and modern concepts fail to explain 'the new situations' which are fast appearing as a result of globalisation and are falling into disrepute. Derrida vehemently talks about deconstruction. He says that the explicit and implicit interpretations of our age, and old macro theories are now put to challenge. Among such theories are some of the reputed theories of patriarchy and patriarchal domination. Women all over the world are challenging the domination exercised by males over the females. The gender problem, which today occupies a sensitive and respectable status in social sciences, challenges the exploitation of the patriarchy. Post-modernist theorists suggest for the deconstruction of patriarchal domination. The women have armed themselves to fight against male chauvinism, the view point of post-modernist is well expressed by Stephen Crook in their post-modernisation work.

Modern societies are characterised by pronounced structural and categorical differentiation at the level of gender. Moreover, the gender system is masculine dominated, that is, it involves the subordination of women by men. Although this is often treated as an undifferentiated structure of patriarchy we preferred to see the masculine gender system of modernization as a process of transformation between two phases, "direct hierarchy and extended-hierarchy."

The approach by post modern thinkers is altogether different, What worries them most is that women should also be given empowerment in the field of consumption. But India is far behind in the realm of post modernity, in fact the problem of empowering women in countries like India involves, a large number of societal sectors

The Indian Experience

The rapid changes that have taken place in the economic, social, scientific and technological and political spheres of development all over the world, have had inevitable repercussions on the role, functions and responsibilities of women in all walks of life. By and large the past few decades have affirmed the transition from traditional to modern and women's development has acquired a high profile in the entire developmental process. Concerted efforts have been made in India to accelerate the pace of women's development programmes in the context of the sheer number's of women who form the backbone of an agricultural economy in transition. The challenge of change and development calls for a constant effort to bring women into the mainstream of eco-enterprenurial and other development activities, A prime requisite is the enlargement of awareness among women and planners, policy makers and development officials are required to pay special attention to the ways and means of accelerating the pace of women's development for their greater role in the development processes.

Power has become relevant today in the context of the upliftment, of woman. The government in India promoted a large number of programmes to improve the status of women and to study the emergence of new status of women; study cells and a large number of NGO'S have been started to promote the cause of women. All our efforts are directed to empower the women-socially, culturally, politically and economically.

Gender relations are of two kinds : biological and socio-cultural. We look at empowerment of women from two basic perspectives one, discrimination and two, lower status in social stratification. The need to empower women in India was being felt right from the sixties of 20th century. The movement increasingly got speeded. It was common to find female foeticide and infanticide. There were political violence, women got marginalised and there was impoverishment of the majority of women within the transforming economy. There were disputes regarding inheritance over property. Even population was explained in terms of the increased procreation of women. Add to it the cases of 'Dowery burning' and ' Injustices' meted against women. It appears that the problem of empowering women has been raised owing to social and historical factors which have rendered women helpless. Power, thus, is specific to time and people. Empowerment of women in India, therefore, has to be seen in a wider context.

A Three Fold Critique of the Women's Empowerment Approach

Viewed from liberal perspective, women's empowerment approach suffers from three fallacies: Exclusionary bias, adversarial orientation and subversive logic (Sharma 2000).

From structural viewpoint, women's empowerment approach is intrinsically psychologistic, astructural and elitist.

From a marxist angle, women's empowerment framework suffers from a sort of non-structuralist bias. This is so because it ignores the importance of existential conditions, including the fact of economic dependency of women on man built into the structure of property relations which are dominated by man. The socialist may argue that women's empowerment perspective has indeed stemmed from a socialist crituque of development strategy and is therefore, appreciative of the role of structural factors in perpetuating gender hierarchy, for without a change in the economic stricture, a change in the power structure remains only a remote possibility. Another problem is that it treats women as a homogeneous category, an undifferetiated mass. It is no secret that movement for women's empowerment has been hijacked by women of higher strata, particularly upper/ middle class and power elites (caplan 1985).

Further, while women power elites favour material empowerment in the form of access in statepower apparatus and economic benefits, the feminist scholars care more for non material, i.e. psychological empowerment in the form of their ability to overcome internalised oppression.

From a cultural point of view, women's empowerment approach can be criticised for its neglect of religion in regulating gender relations and its marked ethnocentrism. (chitnis 1990), (purshothaman, 1998).

The gender relations in India are understandable more in terms of the culture of hierarchy than that of inequality. Some of the notable mechanisms of it are the norms of son preference, daughter is meant for the other family (kanya to paraya dhan), parental obligation to marry off the daughter (kanyadan), riki' as the ideal of wife's fidelity to husband (pativrita), motherhood as the measure of womanhood (matritva). These precisely are the values of patriarchy that the paradigm of women's empowerment seeks to transform. Perhaps a strategy of sabotage from within may be more effective than the one from outside.

The present scenario of women's movement in India (a) either as part of the anti colonial struggle (b) as activism of women's fronts of political parties (c) and as rise of autonomous women's organisations is not all too inspiring. It presents a case of divided unity. It has not been able to grow into a mass movement. In fact, it has not seriously considered the ways and means of dismantling the culture of patriarchy from within nor has it earnestly explored the possibility of drawing men into its fold. Thus the need for gender empowerment instead of empowerment of women vis-a-vis man or vice versa. Because it signifies transformation of gender relations from hierarchical to egalitarian plane rather than just tinkering with women's power position. For this what is actually needed is something more than equality. Hence the relevance of equity for gender empowerment. Equity is about fairness and compensatory justice, it is about enabling provisions to effect, parity in gender relations. It signifies a possibility of transcending the given male standards and creating a new grammar of gender equality. It is to be noted that conscientization is not the only strategy of attitudinal change. Besides several other strategies education and planned socialisation are the two potent instrumentalities of empowerment.

Conclusion

Empowerment is as much a function of structural change as of attitudinal change. Legislation, including constitutional amendments and development planning has its own value despite some of its failings. Strategies have also to be devised to change the culture of gender hierarchy which still has a considerable hold over common man. Finally men need gender sensitization as much as women do to transform the structure of gender relations from hierarchical to egalitarian both at the interpersonal as well as institutional levels of relationships.

REFERENCES

1. Dube, S. C. 1996. 'Vikas Ka Samajshastra', Vani Prakashan, New Delhi.
2. Shiva Vandana 'Ecology & politics of Survival' - Conflicts over natural resources in India, Unites Nations Press 1991, Sage Publications, New Delhi.
3. Sharma, S.L. 2000.' Empowerent without antagonism: A case for reformulation of women's Empowerment approach. Sociological Bulletin Vol. 49, No. 1, March, pp. 19-39.
4. Bandarage, A. 1984, Women in Development: Liberalism and Marxist feminism', Development and change, 15,3, pp. 495-515.
5. Chitnis, S. 1990. 'Feminism: Indian ethos and Indian convictions' in R. Ghadially (ed.) Women in Indian society, New Delhi, sage publication.

6. Deutchman, J. 1991. "The politics of empowerment" women and politics, 11(2), pp. 1-18.
7. Friedmann, J. 1992, Empowerment: The politics of an alternative development, Oxford: Basil Blackwell.
8. Giddens, A. 1984. The constitution of society. Cambridge: Polity Press.
9. Giddens, V. (ed.) 1989. Women, development and empowerment: A Pacific feminist perspective, Kuala Lumpur: Asia and Pacific Development Centre.
10. John, Mary. 1996. "Gender and development in India, 1970s-1990s : Some reflections on the constitutive role of contexts", Economic & Political Weekly, 23, Nov., 3071-77.
11. Kabeer, N. 1990. "Gender, development and training: Raising awareness in development planning", GAADU Newspack No. 14.
12. Kishwar, M. 1990. "Why I do not call myself a feminist?" Mansushi, No. 61.
13. Longwe, Sara. 1991. "Gender awareness: The missing element in the third world development project" in Changing perceptions: Writings on gender development. Oxfam: Oxford.
14. Maguire, P. 19984. Women in development: An alternative analysis, Amherst, MA: Centre for International Education.
15. Mathew, George. 1993. "Beginning of a silent revolution", The Hindu, 18 December.
16. Molyneux, M. 1985. "Mobilization without emancipation: Women's interest, state and revolution in Nicaragua", Feminist Studies, 11, 2, pp. 227-54.
17. Mies, Maria. 1980. Indian women and patriarchy. New Delhi: Vikas
18. Moser, M. 1989. "Gender planning in the third world: Meeting practical and strategic gender needs", World Development, 17,11.
19. Narasimhan, Sakuntala. 1998. Empowering women: An alternative strategy from rural India. New Delhi: Sage Publications.
20. Patel, V. 1985. "Indian women on warpath" in M. Desai (ed.) Reaching for Half the Sky. Baroda: Antar Rashtiya Prakashan.

21. Purushothaman, Sangeetha. 1998. Empowerment of women in India: Grassroots women's networks and the State. New Delhi: Sage Publications.
22. Sharma, K. 1989. "Shared aspirations, fragmented realities, contemporary women's movement in India: Its dialectics and dilemmas". Occasional paper No. 12.
23. Sivaramayya, B. 1984. Inequality and the law. Lucknow Eastern Book Company.
24. Stuadt, K. 1982. "Bureucratic resistance to women's programs: The case of women in development", in Boneparth, E. (de.) Women, power and policy, New York: Pergamon Press, pp. 263-81.
25. Tinker, I. 1990. "The making of a field: Advocate, practitioners, and scholars', in Tinker, I. (ed.) Persistent inequalities, Oxford: Oxford University Press, pp. 27-53.
26. Wallerstein, Immanuel et al. 1997. Open the social sciences: Report of the Gulbenkian Commission on the restructuring of the social sciences. New Delhi: Vistaar Publication.
27. Banu Zenab 2001. "Women Empowerment: Theoretical Thrust" in Indian Journal of Secularism, Vol. 5 No. 1, April-June, pp. 83-94.
28. Beteille Andre, 1999. "Empowerment, Economic and Political Weekly", March, 6-13, p 590.
29. Hoy Dewid Couzens, 1992 Foucault: A Critical Reader, Basil Blackwell.

8

Pattern of Seasonal Unemployment in Uttaranchal Himalayas:

An Empirical Analysis

Dr. A.K. Nauriyal, Dr. M.C. Sati
Dr. R.P. Juyal

Despite several variations in the institutional structure and modes of production ranging from *Jhoom* in the North-Eastern Himalayas to sedentary cultivation in Central and North-western Himalayas, agriculture along with allied activities provide sustenance to majority of the people. Besides, the primary sector activities have far reaching repercussions on the Himalayan ecology, the sustainer of environment and ecology of Indian sub-continent. Due to this overwhelming importance, exhaustive and multidimensional studies on the primary sector of the region are available. Nevertheless, most of these deal with the bio-geographical aspect of the venture. But the problem of Himalayan agriculture, as an economic sector, have been explored marginally. Therefore, in this paper a modest attempt is being made to examine the relatively lesser-explored pattern of employment in agriculture specially in relation to the seasonal rhythm of the venture in Uttaranchal region of the Himalayas.

The Regional and Its Agrarian Structure

The economic structure of Uttaranchal is predominantly

agrarian. As per the census of 1991, 66.32 per cent of main workers are engaged in primary Activities . The monotonous character of the economy is apparent from the fact that only 8.5 per cent workers are engaged in secondary sector activities. Of late, tertiary sector has gained some momentum, there for, 25.15 per cent of the total workforce is employed in it (*Govt. of U.P. 1997*). These statistics of occupational structure are averages of region which has wide variation in resource endowment and level of development Distinctively, different structures of economy are clearly discemible when we disaggregate the region in two parts. The *Southern tip* of the region is consisting of the narrow strip of *Doon valley, Bhabaer and Tarai.* This sub-region is relatively plain endowed with better infrastructural facilities and higher level of urbanisation. This area is spread over only 7.5 per cent of the total geographical area. In this sub-region the net-sown area is relatively high. As in Udham Nagar district, which is the tarai of Himalayan region, the net sown area is well above 40 per cent of the total reported area. The development of irrigation is of the level that as much as about 80 per cent of the net sown area is irrigated. Likewise is the position of the Doon Valley *(Government of U.P., 1997)*. The cropping pattern in this sub-region is highly diversified and commercialized, the agricultural land holding are relatively large and farming is mechanized. Contrary to this the *northern part* of the region, consisting of 92.5 per cent of the total geographical area is rugged mountainous terrain. In this sub region, as an average, 80 per cent of the total main workers are engaged in agriculture. The distribution of arable land is dominated by marginal holdings, which are scattered at least in eight parcels. Irrigation is the most scarce input of agriculture as in some districts like chamoli only 5.2 per cent of net sown area is irrigated, whereas in case of Pithorgarh and Pauri, it is around 8 per cent. In none of the district of the region, excluding Udham Singh Nagar and Doon Valley, the irrigated area is more than 16 per cent of the total net sown area. Therefore vagaries of nature that determine the label of output forced farmers to allot almost entire areable land for, food production because of food security consideration.

The Problem

With this structural backwardness, agriculture being a household venture as in any developing economy, so is in Uttaranchal, is a shelter against economic distress, in which the condition of employment is affected by variety of factors grouped broadly in two categories. First *the overall structural characteristic of the economy,* consisting of technological and institutional aspect of agriculture and other sectors. The impact of imperfection of this factor compels many to join or remain in agriculture workforce when they are seeking job or when they are thrown out of job by other sectors or in other economic distress. Obviously, this implies that some workers could be down out of subsistence farming without reducing the output (*Nurkse, 1966*). Second, *the seasonal rhythm of agricultural operations,* a peculiar characteristic of the sector. It is peculiar because certain agricultural operation are to be completed before beginning or end of the particular season. This rash nature of agriculture activities draws many non-farm workers in the field during peak season, while during slack season even the regular farm workers have to sit idle. This idleness or seasonal unemployment is enforced and inevitable feature of the vocations arises mainly because of the inelastic time pattern of primary sector. Obviously, the aforesaid peculiarities of pattern of employment in agriculture do not get reflected in census data of occupational structure. Census operation norms prescribed a minimum period of employment of six months to enlist a person as main workers in a particular sector.[1] In depth analysis of pattern of employment, therefore, calls for incorporation of these institutional aspects.

The problem of seasonal unemployment is universal phenomena in agriculture, but its magnitude varies with the level of diversification of agriculture, technological and infrastructural advancement. Regions where agriculture operation suffer from the inadequacies of infrastructure such as heavy dependence on rains and is subsistence in nature,[2] seasonal unemployment is bound to be severe. *Ranger Nurkse* has noted that seasonal unemployment is likely to be significant where annual crop cycle e.g. cereal food crops dominates farm activities and where this activity has not developed in a more advanced form such as diary farming. Seasonal unemployment is supposed to be of severe dimensions in the Himalayan region of Uttaranchal because of subsistence nature of it. To assess the magnitude of this problem an empirical study of Okhimath block of Rudraprayag district was conducted in the fall of the year 1999.

The Sample-Okhimath Block

Situated in the north-eastern part of Garhwal Division of Uttranchal, Okhimath block is a part of tehsil Okhimath, district Rudrerprayag. The elevation of block varies from 1200 meter mean sea level in the South to North, North-west and North-east forming the Chaukamba peak-7138 meters. The abrupt change in elevations within a short distance of about 80 kilometers along with various localised factors, like the aspect of particular locality in relation to higher Himalayan ranges, make the climate of the block very complex and diversified varying from temperate to arctic type. This physiographic characteristic puts the block in a distinct category of agro-climatic resource zone, in which by and large, spatial peculiarities of agro-resource endowments of Uttaranchal region get represented.

Similar to the condition prevalent in other parts of Uttaranchal, cultivation in the area is not possible without terracing. Due to physiographic constraints, arable land and irrigation are the scarce inputs. In Okimath block only 2912 hectares have been reported as net sown area (7.9 per cent of the total reported area) out of which 68 hectares (about 2 per cent of the net sown area) is irrigated. It is pertinent to note here that the availability of aforsaid two inputs viz. areiable land and irrigation declines with increase in altitude. The land distribution pattern is dominated by large number of marginal farmers as 78 per cent of the agricultural holdings are of below one hectare, and they acount for 30 per cent of the total areable land. With this meager arable land and dominance of marginal farmers, about 94 per cent of the total cropped area is under cereals in which millets account for about one third of the total copped area (*Govt. of U.P., 1997*).

In demographic dynamics, this block is an ideal sample of rural Uttaranchal Himalaya. The total population of the block is 38646 people. The sex ratio is 991 female per 1000 of male, just equal to regional average. Similarly, male and female literacy figures are 66.23 per cent and 32.74 per cent of the respective totals. The economy of the block is monotonous. The primary sector alone employs 81 per cent of the total main workers. Agricultural activities account for 80 per cent of the total workers, there are no industrial enterprises, household or other, of any significance. Besides primary activities, the tertiary sector, consisting mainly of government employees, teachers and workers engaged in tourism/pilgrimage[3] activities have some significance as about 15.50 per cent of total workers are employed in this sector. (*Census,1991*).

Methodology

To assess the extent of seasonal unemployment in Okimath block, a survey was conducted in the months of October-November 1999[4]. The magnitude of seasonal unemployment varies with the agro-resource endowment and infrastructural facilities available to individual cultivator. Therefore, stratified sampling technique was preferred to random to give due representation to these factors and to incorporate the varying physiographic and climatic condition, *all the 135 inhabited villages of the block* were grouped in 6 *eco-environmental and resource Tones.*[5] thereafter, villages were arranged in each zone depending upon the accessibility to vehicles plying (pucca) roads[6]. The delineation of the area in accordance to the physiographic zones is specifically done to weight the environmental impact in the process of decision making and population pressure on land. Likewise farmer's accessibility to input supply and extension centre plays a critical role in the input use pattern and crop choice. Therefore, to give weightage to this dimension, the villages were grouped according to their accessibility.

After stratifying all the village of the study area in the two starata table, vertical axis representing the eco-environmental zone and horizontal axis denoting distance of villages from vehicular road. In all 12 villages were selected randomly from each strata.[7] From this first Unit of sampling (FUS) i.e. village the second and ultimate Unit of sampling (UUS) i.e. households were selected. For selecting the UUS first of all the land holding of households were obtained from revenue records for each selected village. The land holding were initially grouped in two board categories viz. marginal holding and above marginal holdings. But due to the overwhelming number of marginal holding and meagure number of small farmers the above-referred two fold division i.e. marginal and above marginal holdings become irrelevant. Therefore, holding were further sub-divided into the following categories and modal size of holding for each categories were calculated[8].

The household possessing modal land holding in each category were randomly selected for investigation. In this process 184 *households in all were selected for investigation.* Out of these 184 households 100 households were the owners of 15 nalies of land; 54 households possess land 30 nalies, 25 household possessed 50 nalies each and only 5 house holds have land ownership of 72 nalies each. Among these households a questionnaire was administered.

Table 1: Okhimath Block: Model Size of Land Holding

Sl.No.	*Category ownership of land*	*Model size of hildings*	*Percentage of house hold in each category to total households*
1.	0-20 Nali	15	52
2.	20-40 Nali	30	27
3.	40-60 Nali	0	18
4.	Above 60 Nali	72	03

Note: Nali is a vemacular measurement unit of land. One Nali is approximately equal to 196 Sq. mts thereby 51 Nali = 1 hectare.

The questionnaire was carved to sought information about allotment of land in different uses, area under different crops and their rotation[9], workers employed along with their gender-composition and days of work in each crop. Specific questions were asked whether the household employ hired labour, or whether the migrated family member(s) join the farming activities during the peak season.

The formidable problem that arose in the statistical analysis of the data collected was of varying size of labour force in relation to every model holding, as total workforce and according to the gender composition. Thus to narrow down the number of varying size of labour force, model size of labourforce according to gender composition were calculated for the model holdings identified in table 1. Except the case of modal holding size of 72 nalies, one male and one female workers were found in all size of land holdings.

The information obtained in this process were tabulated crop and gender wise for each modal holding. In the Rabi crop the days of employment happens to be less in every modal holding for worker of either gender because the farm operations[10] are less and restricted to preparation of fields i.e. clearing of bushes and picking of pebbles, plaguing and leveling of fields, sowing, harvesting, husking and storage.

Although, the days of work are less in the rabi crops but, the hours of work are longer. Because the prepration for fields for ploughing and levelling of fields is to be done intensively before the out break of winters. Likewise the harvesting is also to be done quickly as the fields have to

Table 2: Okimath Block: The Modal size of Labor force and its Gender Composition

Size of Labour Force	*Male*	*Female*
2	1	1
3	1	2
4	2	2
5	2	3

be vacated for sowing of Kharif crops before the onset of extreme summer. In Kharif crops, the days of work happens to be more because of the larger number of crops and more due to onset of monsoon which causes growth of weeds in the fields. These weeds have to be cleared regularly by harrowing and weeding manually. In the Kharif crops, the number of days of female workers happens to be more in all of size of holdings. The days of working in Rabi and Kharif crops for each modal holding and as per the modal size of labour force are shown in table 3.

After obtaining the days of employment in Rabi and Kharif crops in each modal holding according to the gender composition of workforce, the total days of employment were calculated. From this the total days of seasonal unemployment were derived simply by subtracting the days of employment from 365 days. The results are shown in table 4.

Result and Discuassion

To get a general trend of seasonal unemployment in the area, geometric mean[11] of the seasonal unemployment in the modal holding of 15 Nails, 30 Nalies were calculated. For the

Table 3: Okimath Block: Days of Employment in Different Crops by Modal Size of Holding, 1998-99

Modal size of Holding (in Nali)	*Model size of Labor Force and Days employment in Rabi Corps*								*Modal size of Labor Force and Days of employment in Kharif Corps*							
	Two workers		*Three workers*		*Four workers*		*Five workers*		*Two workers*		*Three workers*		*Four workers*		*Five workers*	
	M	F	M	F	M	F	M	F	M	F	M	F	M	F	M	F
	1	1	1	2	2	2	2	3	1	1	1	2	2	2	2	3
15	50	80	40	60	30	40	NA	NA	70	180	55	105	45	90	NA	NA
30	15	90	60	80	NA	NA	40	90	90	200	85	159	NA	85	65	110
50	100	130	80	100	NA	NA	40	80	135	210	110	165	NA	NA	60	120
72	NA	NA	90	130	70	100	50	85	NA	NA	130	215	110	160	80	130

M=Male, F=female, N.A. available

Table 4: Okimath Block: Days of Employment in Different Crops by Modal Size of Holding, 1998-99

Modal size of holding (in Nail)	*Model size of labour Force Total Days of Employment*								*Modal size of Labor Force Total days of Seasonal unemployment*							
	Two workers		*Three workers*		*Four workers*		*Five workers*		*Two workers*		*Three workers*		*Four workers*		*Five workers*	
	M	F	M	F	M	F	M	F	M	F	M	F	M	F	M	F
	1	1	1	2	2	2	2	3	1	1	1	2	2	2	2	3
15	120	260	95	165	75	130	NA	NA	245	105	250	200	290	235	NA	NA
30	165	290	145	210	NA	NA	105	200	200	75	220	155	NA	NA	260	165
50	235	340	190	265	NA	NA	100	200	130	25	175	100	NA	NA	NA	NA
72	NA	NA	210	345	260	260	130	215	NA	NA	155	20	185	105	233	150

M= male, F=female, N.A. Not available

modal workforce of 2 workers, 1 male and 1 female each, is available for these holdings alone. This statistical treatment reveals that in a year as a whole an average agriculture worker has to sit idle for 145 days. For a male worker the days of unemployment are as high as 175 days whereas for female worker, days of unemployment are only 147 days in a year. Here it is important to mention, that if a worker has worked even for a single hour in her/his fields or as hired labour, she/he was considered gainfully employed for that day. This is simply because agriculture practices are generally combined with animal husbandry and sheep rearing. Some of the activities of these two ventures are so mixed that they can not be categorized separately. For instance collecting fodder and fuel from the field entails cutting bushes and weeding grasses etc. which are also activities to prepare fields for plaguing or protecting the crops from weeds.

The above referred tables reveal that the incidence of seasonal unemployment and size of holding is negatively related, as with increase in size of holding, days of seasonal unemployment tends to decline. This decline is more for male workers than female. The reason for these characteristics are broadly rooted in the behavioural settings and value premises of agriculture work, and to some extent to the economies of scale. Generally, in the study area male perform agriculture operation which require either hard labour or are carried out with the help of animals like ploughing of fields and harrowing the crops. These activities require a shorter duration, women perform all those activities which are spread over a relatively larger period and require precision like preparation of field, weeding of crops, cutting of crops, husking and storage of the produce. For these reasons the days of seasonal unemployment for female workers are just less than one month, in land holding of 72 Nalies, whereas in the same holding the days of unemployment for male workers are about 5 months.

Another important inference drawn form the aforesaid data is that seasonal unemployment for male workers tends to decline more sharply with increase in size of holdings, than they decrease for female workers. The reason for this discrepancy lies in the opportunities of agriculture diversification and generation of marketable serplus on larger holdings. These possibilities offer some temptation to male workers to take up agricultural work for monetary income.

Applicability

The seasonal unemployment studies are immensely valuable for employment planning, especially in rural areas where additional employment opportunities are to be provided during slack seasons under employment guarantee scheme for marginal and landless laborers. In case of this study area, seasonal unemployment is more acute in Rabi season (winter). Incidentally this is also the period when employment in other sectors like tourism and pilgrimage cease to exist due to closer of the holy shrines. Therefore, it is more appropriate to launch employment guarantee programmes during these months.

Although, the area has considerable cultivable wasteland but due to infrastructural inadequacies it is difficult to bring this under plough. Moreover much of the arable land cultivable waste is beyond eco-environmental safe limits of 30° slopes. Cultivation on such land is not free from the apprehensions of environmental degradation.

Similarly the opportunity to intensify and diversify agriculture are also limited. During the course of investigation, it was observed that the area is well exposed to modern agronomic practices. The cultivators are well aware of utility of HYV and fertilizers and of allotting of land for cash crop and horticulture. But, the scattered and tiny holdings along with environment constraints and inadequacies of infrastructure militate against the process of diversification of agriculture. This study therefore, makes clear that employment opportunities have to generate outside the primary sector. This constraint become apparently more clear from the observation that even owners of large holdings suffer from chronic seasonal unemployment.

Notes

1. In census of 1981 a person who had worked for six month or 183 days in preceding year, was considered as main worker. The same definition was followed in the census of 1991.
2. Subsistence farming is the farming in which farmers consume most which they produce or in other words it is the level of consumption which is fixed and marketable surplus is residual.
3. Pilgrimage is an age old profession of Uttaranchal Himalayas. It has five word renowned Hindu shrines of *Kedamath, Badrinath, Gangotri, Yamnotri and Sikh Shrine of Hemkunt Sahib.* The Kedarnath shrine in Okhimath Block, is one of the Panch Kedars, five shrines of lord Shiva. namely, *Kedamath, Tungnath, Madhymaheswar and Rudmath.*
4. October-November month were preferred for carrying out field study, because the farm activities are slack in these months after harvesting Kharif crops and sowing Rabi crops. The pilgrimage activities also come to temporary halt, after the closer of the shrine for winter. Therefore, The inhabitants of the block can afford leisure, to respond to survey.
5. On the basis of the floristic pattern, climate, habitiation, availability of arable land and accessibility, following eco-environmental and resource zones have been delineated in Okhimath block, the area lying below 1400 meters between 1400-1800, 1800-2200, 2200-2600, 2600-3000,

3000-3400 and 3400 meters and above. (Juyal R.P., *Micro Level Planning for Rural Development in Grahwal Himalayas,* unpublished ph.D. Thesis, Garhwal University, Srinagar, Garhwal, 1984).

6. The distance cariterion i.e. accessibility of villages from vehicular road, has been adopted by various development agencies for planning rural infrastructrual and services. The usual criterion is as follows: villages at a distance of less than 1 Km from vehicular road, 1 to 3 Km., 3 to 5 Km., 5 Km. and above.

7. The number of villages selected for sample survey were less than the number of strata formed because in many strata on single village surfaced. the village in which investigation were carried are enlisted below:

Altitude in meter	*Accessibility from vehicular Road*			
	Less then 1 Km	*1 to 3 Km*	*3 to 5 Km*	*5 Km and above*
less then 1400	Bhasari	—	Parkindi	Lawara
1400-1800	phata	painj	Anderwadi Kawitha	
1800-2200	Gauri Kund	Krokhi Malli	—	Chaumasi
2200-2600	Trijugi Narayan	—	—	—
2600-3000	—	—	—	Tosi
3000-3600	—	—	—	—

8. Mode has been preferred to other measure of central tendencies mainly because of its characteristic of most frequent occurrence and physical presence as a variable in the universe.

9. The farmer of Uttaranchal have unique cropping pattern. The total available land of the village is divided into two parts part A and part B. Thse

parts are referred as *Sars*. During Monsoon both *Sars* have Khariff crops. Let us suppose *sar* A has crops of paddy along with other millets like Sawan and Kauni and Sar B has crops of Ragi, Soya beans and other legumes. After harvesting the crop of paddy from *Sar* A by late September the field are immediately prepared for sowing Rabi crops of wheat, oilseeds and masoor which will be reaped by May But after harveting the Rabi crops from *Sar* B by mid October the fields are left fallow till February. In the month of March Paddy is sown in these fields of *Sar* B. Where as in the fields of *Sar* A, Rabi crops are standing which will be barvested by May and the fields will be utilized for showing Kharif crops of Ragi. The above mentioned crop rottion has been shown in the following chart:

Okhimath Block: Crop Rotation

Sar A			*Sar B*		
Crop	*Sowing Season*	*Harvesting Season*	*Crop*	*Sowing Season*	*Harvesting Season*
Paddy	March-April	Late September	Raghi	Mid May	Mid October
Wheat	October	May	Fallow from Mid October to February		
Ragi	Mid May	Mid October	Paddy	March-April	Late September
Fallow from Mid October to February			Wheat	October	May
Paddy	March-April	Late September	Ragi	Mid May	Mid October

REFERENCES

Government of India, *Census of India 1991*, office of the Registrar General, New Delhi, Census Handbook of District Chamoli (obtained from NIC).

Government of Uttar Pradesh, *Uttrakhand ki Sankhikeya Diary*, State Planning Institute, Lucknow, 1997.

Government of Uttar Pradesh, *Draft IX, five year plan, 1997-2000,* Uttaranchal sub-plan vol. (1), Uttaranchal Vikash, Lucknow.

Government of Uttar Pradesh, *Sankhikeya, Patrika Janpad Chmoli,* 1997, District Statistical Office Gopeswar, Chamoli.

Nurkse, Rangnar, *Problems of Capital Formation in Under Developed Countries* Oxford, 1966.

9

Community Assets and Employment Generation under JRY in Karnataka:

A Dolorous Performance

M. Mahadeva

Of all the public policy on rural employment and poverty alleviation (Raghav Gaiha, 1991; Vyans and Pradeep Bhargava, 1995) Jawahar Rozgar Yojana (JRY) is considered as unique and prominent scheme in India. Because all other initiatives were by and large beneficiary oriented aiming at uplifting the poor families with the help of remunerative assets thus created, skill development or improvement, etc. Secondly community based assets creation was largely confined to either drought prone areas or most backward regions. There was a total lack on the part of the public concern to develop community based assets in the country side. Further in terms of implementation also (devolution of resources, decision making and peoples' participation etc.), JRY is unlike other schemes. Decentralised Governments (Zilla, Taluk and Village Panchayats) have been given a free hand in evolving the projects needed to the community as a whole as well as in prioritising the resource allocations. This means, although State Government share the matching grants with the Central Government, they have been given an overall supervisory role. Rural people are made to take part directly in decision making in regard to prioritising the developmental activities which are beneficial to the rural community. In addition to this, selection of Scheduled Caste and Scheduled Tribe beneficiaries for the directly benefiting assets creation out of the earmarked funds of 22.5 per cent of JRY funds also rest with the rural community. A major chunk of the public resources (over 70 per cent) under JRY was given to village panchayats for generation of employment and for asset creation.

All said and done the evaluation has brought to the fore many disappointing realities in the implementation of JRY through out the country (GOI, 1995; Neelakantan, 1993). First of all, there has been a very poor coverage of the poorest of the poor in the JRY works, besides generation of limited employment opportunities and income to the JRY workers owing to inadequate public investment. Apart from this lack of uniformity in the impact of JRY across different States in the country, despite following a common implementation strategy has brought to the fore the need for the consideration of socio-economic realities especially the levels of poverty at the regional levels for allocation of funds. Some of the states have especially even performed very badly in terms of the above parameters. Karnataka is such state in which case the impact of JRY on employment and income is far from satisfaction owing to erosion of investment over the years. Fragmentation of resources due to a large number of villages per panchayat is an added dimension of the poor performance.

Data Base and Methodology

The analysis in the paper is based on the data collected from the secondary as well as primary sources. The statistical information in regard to performance of JRY in Karnataka has been drawn from the Second Concurrent Evaluation of JRY of Government of India. Similarly to understand district wise investment pattern under JRY and physical assets and employment creation, the data provided by the Department of Rural Development and Panchayati Raj, Government of Karnataka has been used. In addition, primary data on various aspects of JRY has been collected from a number of selected village panchayats. Tested Questionnaire has been used to elicit information. Discussions with panchayat members and JRY workers also form the basis for analysis.

The Second Concurrent Evaluation of JRY has selected 40 blocks in the State at the rate of two blocks from each of the twenty districts. From each selected block a sample of five village panchayats was selected to collect information on JRY. Thus in total the survey selected two hundred villages for detailed investigation at the rate of five villages from each block. Further for primary survey, eight villages have been randomly selected from four different blocks spread over to four districts including the two that are considered most backward for the purpose of implementation of Intensified Jawahar Rozgar Yojana (IJRY) in the State.

Objectives

For the reasons stated elsewhere, this paper is a moderate attempt to present a number of hard realities with regard to JRY in Karnataka. The specific objectives of the paper are: (a) to examine the performance of JRY in Karnataka as captured by the Second Concurrent Evaluation, (b) to analyse the investment pattern under JRY and IJRY across different districts for two periods, (c) to throw light on employment generation, asset creation including wages and finally to draw inferences for further policy making to make JRY more effective in rural areas. The paper is classified into four parts. Part one deals with important findings of the survey with regard to JRY in Karnataka. The second part deals with the most crucial aspect of investment pattern across different districts between 1989-90 to 1993-94 and 1994-95 to 1997-98 for implementation of JRY. Field insights of JRY from the selected villages are presented in the third section, which will be followed by concluding observations in the last section. These issues are crucial from the focal point of making JRY more purposeful.

I

JRY IN KARNATAKA : A DOLOROUS SITUATION

To begin with, it is better to characterise the gram panchayats in Karnataka as they play a major role[1] in implementing the JRY in rural areas. The survey points out that more than 92 per cent of the heads of the panchayats were untrained and all of them belong to non-social groups (other than scheduled castes and tribes). Being male, a large majority of panchayat heads are qualified graduates (61.54 per cent) followed by intermediate and matric level educational qualifications. This apart, more than 92 per cent of the panchayat heads are agriculturists with majority of them owing agricultural lands between 2 and 4 hectares. It is also true that there is no single instance where a landless person is heading the panchayat. These instances confirm that the process of bringing weaker sections (mainly landless social groups) into the political stream at the grass root level is yet to take a proper shape. In other words, power concentration among the upper castes as well as land owing classes has remained unchecked. This has upon the result into the increasing dependence of large segments of the rural poor privileged groups. It is deny further argued that power concentration not only denied opportunities to rural poor in the political process but also divert the benefits of development works and anti-poverty programmes towards powerful groups (Raghav Gaiha, et al., 1998).

Karnataka is one of the few states where bureaucracy continues to play a major role in executing the JRY works. The survey clearly pointed out that, of the 2010 completed JRY works (on an average of ten works per panchayat) almost all of them were executed by the panchayat secretary.

Whereas the average of intervention of bureaucracy is only 24 per cent under JRY at the all India level. In this regard some of the implementational shortcomings were also noticed during the field survey. In a large number of cases most of the JRY works (especially repair and road construction, construction works) were executed either by the elected panchayat members themselves or their close relatives on piece work basis. Maintenance of muster roll of registrants is hardly adhered to. Further, the effectiveness of any programme in general and JRY in particular is also attributed to both. The number of families below poverty line and number of villages per panchayat. Surprisingly Karnataka is one of the few states with highest number of poor families and the highest number of villages per panchayat. There are 1274 families below poverty line and each panchayat has to cater to the needs of 13 villages as against 451 families and 4 villages of the national average. This is 3 times higher than the average. This is perhaps one of the reasons for the fragmentation of resources under JRY. As a result of thin availability of resources and high incidence of poor families, the coverage of poor families (<Rs. 11,000 income per annum) under JRY employment was only one-fourth, which is lower than the national average of over 31 per cent and generation of less number of employment.

Receiving allocated funds at the right time to exeute the designated developmental expenditure is an important component in minimising the delays in work completion. Of the two sources of funds (first unspent balance of previous year and second the current years' allocation) for implementation of JRY, the survey indicates that a good share of over 18 per cent of the resources came as uninitiated money of the previous year. The field information unutilised provided conclusion that panchayats received a large chunk of the current year allocation only at the fag end of the financial year. This has not only delayed the completion of the works under JRY but also led to substandard works as the same were to be completed within the given financial year. Survey data also strengthen this argument that the percentage of delayed works under JRY in Karnataka is more as compared to all India level and shortage of funds as well as delay in receiving funds by the panchayats have been the reasons attributed. What is further disheartening is the availability of funds under JRY. It is as meagre as Rs. 0.22 lakhs per village as against Rs. 0.31 lakhs in the country. If 22.5per cent is taken out for works which directly benefit the SCs/STs compulsorily the effective availability of funds for community benefiting developmental works is only a little over Rs. 0.17 lakhs. Further if it is shared between materials as well as wages at the suggested rate it work out to Rs. 6,800 and Rs. 10,200 respectively. With this approximately 392 mandays of employment could be created roughly for 49 persons for 8 days in each village.

Annual income, occupation and the social status are the important determinants for the selection of the target groups for JRY works. These determinants are employed mainly to give priority to the most deserving and to adequately represent acutely poor families. The target group includes landless labourers, marginal farmers scheduled castes and scheduled tribes and those who have a family income of less than Rs. 11,000 per annum which are considered to be the highly deprived and target groups in rural areas. In regard to the representation of the designated target groups in JRY works, the position of Karnataka is disturbing in the sense that the target group account to only 66 per cent which is far below the national average of 82 per cent. Rest or one-third of the JRY works have been garnered by the undistinguished non-poor beneficiaries who have a family income of more than Rs. 11,000. It is further disturbing to note that the representation of acutely poor families with less than Rs. 6400 income per annum is very negligible at 24 per cent in Karnataka as against an average representation of 32 per cent in India. It can be noted that panchayats being the principal agency of implementation dissuasion of non-poor from the JRY works is perplexing for two obvious reasons. First at times of labour scarcity (especially vulnerable groups) panchayats are forced to employ the non-targeted workers in order to complete the ongoing works within the time schedule. Second, there is a tendency on the part of the non-poor workers to accept the locally available works even at lower levels of wages. Panchayat members have got to accommodate the non-poor families as they have their own interests. Yet another determinant factor increasingly gaining importance in selection of beneficiaries is the landlessness. Karnataka has been in the forefront by accommodating landless labourers upto 80 per cent of the JRY total workers. However the representation of occupationally ineligibles (other workers) are eight times more than the average. There exists hardly any difference in the representation of the social groups.

In regard to the community assets creation under JRY, overriding importance has been given to the construction of roads, drainages, building works. These works account to 60 per cent of the total expenditure. SC/ST benefiting works[2] constitute to around 18 per cent. These expenditures are certainly higher than the average expenditure on assets creation excepting construction of road works. Expenditure on SC/ST works is higher by three times. Eventually construction of these assets have generated 60 per cent of the total employment. However, the quality of the works undertaken under JRY is questionable as a large majority suffer from lack of quality materials used. The field experience concludes that most of the buildings and the roads have been defaced and washed off in the rains within a very short period. The use of the substandard materials owing to inadequate funds has been a prominent reason for the same.

The wage payment under JRY works is not only miserable but contemptible in Karnataka. The State has paid lowest wages for JRY works. The wages paid for unskilled male and female as well as skilled workers were not only lower than the local wage during the lean/off season periods but also national averages (Rs. 22). Wages were paid at Rs. 16.06 and Rs. 16.04 for unskilled male and female and Rs. 30.20 for skilled labourers under JRY as against Rs. 26.17, Rs. 19.58 and Rs. 62.43 of local wage rates. This leaves a difference of Rs. 10.11, Rs. 3.54 and Rs. 32.23 respectively. In other words JRY paid wage rate were lower by 38 and 18 per cent in case of unskilled male and female and is around 52 per cent in the case of skilled labourers. This apart, JRY wages were also lower than the national average by Rs. 10.02 (per cent) Rs. 8.47 (34 per cent) for unskilled male and female workers and Rs. 16.01 (35 per cent) for skilled workers. Owing to the lower wages paid, the incremental income to the families was anything around Rs. 1300 for unskilled male and female and around Rs. 2400 for skilled labourers, which is only 12 and 22 per cent of the poverty line income. Lack of knowledge on the part of a large majority of JRY workers about the minimum wages (updated), JRY and local wages, have prompted to accept the lower wages. Violation of guidelines in regard to displaying details about JRY especially the amount received, wages to be paid etc. has further prompted the payment of lower wage rate.

II

INVESTMENT-ASSET CREATION-EMPLOYMENT GENERATION : DISAPPOINTING REALITIES

Investment Pattern

Though Central Government plays a very significant role in investing a large share of the funds, State Governments at the same time also play an equally important role not only in contributing their respective share but also by implementing JRY. The allocation from the state to the districts is made on the basis of the proportion of rural SC/ST population in a district to total rural SC/ST proportion in the state and the inverse of per capita production of agricultural workers with equal weights. In Karnataka, the pattern of investment under JRY across districts for two periods (i.e., 1989-90 to 1993-94 or the first five years and 1994-95 to 1997-98 or the second period) is presented in table 1. The reason for bifurcation for period is to observe the change that has taken place during the second period with the introduction of Intensified Jawahar Rozgar Yojana (IJRY)[3] during 1994-95. According to the sub-scheme backward identified districts get an additional allocation of 20 per cent. The distribution of investment under JRY largely varies as there are differences across districts in the parameters employed for this purpose. But as such, the increase in investment during the second period is only a marginal or 1.26 per cent. This is very clear from the table that average annual investment rose from Rs. 3184.87 lakhs in 1989-90 to 1993-94 to Rs. 3224.88 lakhs during 1994-95 to 1997-98. However in the case of a very few districts the average investment has increased phenomenally during the second period. For instance, the increase is over 70 per cent in the case of Kodagu, followed by Uttar Kannada (55.89 per cent), bidar (35.93 per cent), Mysore (17.99 per cent) and Chikmagalur (14.93 per cent). Similarly in the case of a few others, the increase is only a negligible. But 8 out of 20 districts have registered a negative growth rate in the sense that there has been an erosion of allocation during the second period. Mandya and Belgaum have had a highest erosion of allocation by-13.69 per cent and -11.46 per cent respectively. What is further disturbing is the erosion of regular investment among the identified IJRY districts (Kolar, Tumkur, Chitradurga, Bijapur, Dharwar, Gulbarga, Bellary and Bidar) let alone the additional investment. Under IJRY the allocation should have been increased for these districts by at least 20 per cent or there should have been an additional outlay at Rs. 7.3 crores per district on an average (Parameshwaran Iyer, 1994). but in reality, not only this did not happen but there has been an erosion of allocation in half

Table 1: Investment Pattern under JRY in Karnataka

District	*Investment During*			*Average expenditure*		
	1989-90 to 1993-94	*1994-95 to 1997-98*	*% charge*	*Per panchayat*	*per village*	*Effective expenditure for direct employment*
Bangalore urban	1752.38	1906.15	8.77	3.53	0.59	0.46
Bangalore rural	2840.60	2647.82	-6.79	2.66	0.38	0.30
Kolar*	5114.10	4708.56	-7.92	3.57	0.40	0.31
Tumkur*	4587.66	4289.36	-6.50	3.07	0.38	0.30
Chitradurga*	4378.61	4214.77	-3.74	2.26	0.56	0.43
Shimoga	2350.03	2597.86	10.55	2.13	0.35	0.27
Mysore	5257.61	4311.77	17.99	2.94	0.59	0.46
Mandya	2003.01	1728.78	-13.69	1.78	0.30	0.23
Hassan	2513.72	2666.21	6.07	2.22	0.25	0.19
Chikmagalur	1878.43	2182.89	14.93	1.99	0.40	0.31
Kodagu	9.9.68	1549.75	70.36	2.76	0.92	0.71
Dakshina Kannada	2425.28	2392.04	-1.37	1.52	0.76	0.59

(Table Contd....)

(Table 1: Contd...)

District	Investment During 1989-90 to 1993-94	Investment During 1994-95 to 1997-98	% charge	Average expenditure Per panchayat	Average expenditure per village	Effective expenditure for direct employment
Belgaum	3524.20	3120.35	-11.46	1.53	0.76	0.59
Bijapur*	4555.47	4060.26	-8.68	2.66	0.89	0.69
Dharwar*	4232.75	4440.6	4.91	2.19	0.55	0.43
Uttar Kannada	1081.71	1685.52	55.81	1.38	0.23	0.18
Gulbarga*	5003.98	5313.88	6.19	3.41	0.85	0.66
Raichur	4070.32	4429.13	8.82	3.14	0.63	0.49
Bellary*	3051.78	3205.6	5.04	3.68	1.23	0.95
Bidar*	2146.04	2917.27	35.93	3.18	1.06	0.82
Average	3184.87	3224.88	1.26	2.50	0.50	0.39

Note: * Intensified Jawahar Rozgar Yoznar districts.

Source: Compiled from the data provided by the Government of Karnataka, Rural Development and Panchayati Raj, 1997-98.

of these districts. Bijapur being the topper has the highest erosion by-8.68 followed by Kolar (-7.92 per cent), Tumkur (-6.5 per cent) and Chitradurga (-3.74 per cent). Constrast to this, except Bidar which has registered an increased allocation by 35.94 per cent, in all other IJRY districts, the outlays increased is by and large in par with the general increase owing to inflation.

Further similar trend can also be observed in the case of expenditure per panchayat and per village under JRY. Since each panchayat consists of 5 villages on an average, the expenditure per panchayat is Rs. 2.50 lakhs, although a number of districts have exceeded the same. While per village expenditure depends on the number of villages per panchayat, more the number of villages less will be the availability of funds/expenditure and vice-versa. The average expenditure per village is Rs. 0.50 lakhs. But further, more important is the effective expenditure[4] for direct employment activities. Here again in a good number of districts, the net available funds for employment generation is less than the average of Rs. 0.39 lakhs. But as a result of the less number of villages per panchayat the effective expenditure in villages is higher than the average in districts like Bellary, Bidar, Kodagu, Bijapur and Gulbarga etc.

Assets Creation

Under JRY, a wide range of developmental works have been completed mainly to fulfil the primary objective of employment generation in rural areas. While doing so, construction works have been given overriding priority as they have a direct relationship with employment opportunities and the assets created are by and large community based. This does not mean that other assets are not community based and have no relationship with employment opportunities. But by and large, these assets are more beneficial to the individual families. Such assets can be identified as works related to minor irrigation, soil conservation, housing and related works including development of house sites. Not withstanding the same, under construction works, rural link roads school buildings, other buildings (like community centres for revenue purposes) community latrines have been very prominent during the period 1989-90 to 1993-94. These works account to a majority in the total as these works were preferred by the rural communities. It has been argued that rural link roads are often selected under any employment programme for higher response of the poor in such works and there is greater opportunity for corruption and malpractices in such works (Jos Chathukulam and V.K. Kurien, 1995). As can be seen in table 2, more or less the same works were taken up on a large scale even during the second i.e., 1994-95 to 1996-97, although social forestry and development works (mainly land development for house sites formation purposes) have been given priority over the other works.

Further erosion of investment under JRY during the second period has affected the asset creation process in rural areas. During the period, there has been a reduction in the number of public works. Especially in certain sectors, the decline is drastic. The table clearly shows that the average asset creation across the various sectors is significantly low during the second period as compared to the first period. Soil conservation works being an important activity under agriculture has a highest negative growth rate by -76 per cent. The average hectares brought under social forestry during the second period was only 1330 as against 5560 hectares in the first period. This is followed by -36 per cent in the construction of school buildings, -35 per cent in link roads construction, -30 per cent in the construction of community or other buildings and so on. However, minor irrigation, village tanks and construction of panchayat offices works have maintained constant growth. Particularly construction of community latrine works have increased by 141 per cent. Similarly other works' have also been increased phenomenally by more than two times.

Table 2: Physical Assets Created under JRY in Karnataka 1989-90 to 1996-97

Sl. No.	*Works*	*1989-90 to 1993-94* total	*Average per year*	*1994-95 to 1996-97* Total	*Average per year*
1.	Social Forestry				
	(a) Area covered (Hec)	35854	7171	16369	5456
2.	Agriculture (hect)				
	(a) Minor irrigation	1038	208	1261	420
	(b) Soil conservation	27800	5560	3989	1330
3.	Construction works				
	(a) Rural roads (kms)	63360	12672	24334	8111
	(b) Village tanks (Nos.)	2011	402	1545	515
	(c) Houses (Nos)	31255	6251	18283	6094
	(d) Panchayat offices (Nos)	1125	225	1057	352
	(e) Mahila mandals (Nos)	1355	271	646	215
	(f) Community latrines (Nos)	77630	1526	11022	3674
	(g) MWS wells (Nos)	11091	2218	8001*	
	(h) IAY houses (Nos)	32365	6473	13911*	
	(i) Drinking water wells (Nos)	3704	741	1921	640
	(j) School buildings (Nos)	16525	3305	6305	2102
	(k) Construction of buildings (Nos)	15688	3138	6547	2182
4.	Development works				
	(a) Land (hect)	4822	964	10531	3510
	(b) House sites (hect)	481	96	1635	546
5.	Other works (Nos)	64824	12965	134455	44818

Note: * Figures are for 1994-95 only as MWS & IAY have become independent schemes from 1995-96 onwards.

Source: Compiled from the data provided by Department of RDPR, Government of Karnataka.

Employment Generation

Yet another noticeable impact of erosion of allocation under JRY is the significant fall in the number of man-days of employment during the second period. The overall employment generated has fallen considerably from 23 million mandays in the first period to 13.61 million mandays in the second period. This drop is around -41 per cent. The average annual mandays of employment has also reduced from 4.59 million to 3.40 million or -26 per cent during the period under review. Across districts the fall is even higher than the average in half of the districts although in a few districts, the average employment growth is positive. Especially in the case of Shimoga the average negative growth rate is more than -55 per cent followed by Mandya (-47.72 per cent), Mysore (-45.25 per cent) and Belgaum (-41.35 per cent). Even not a single of the IJRY districts could escape from the fall in average number of man-days of employment. More so in the case of Bijapur, Dharwar and Kolar, the drop is over one-third. In addition to the fall in the number of employment under JRY, there has also been a drop in the participation of the poorer sections in the JRY workers. The same has dropped from 0.57 million during 1989-90 to 1993-94 to 0.43 million in 1994-95 to 1996-97.

III

FIELD INSIGHTS ON JRY: BEYOND THE GUIDE LINES

At the outset, JRY in selected villages has been implemented without following the scheme guidelines strictly owing to predominantly inadequate public investment. In each of the selected eight gram panchayats, the average number of villages covered by a panchayat work out to 5 to 6 excepting in Dakshin Kannada where the coverage is only 2 to 3 villages per panchayat. In fact villages covered by each panchayat of the selected districts is even higher than the all India average of 4. More villages per panchayat has led to fragmentation of the resources, taking

Table 3 : Employment Generation under JRY

(In lakh mandays)

Districts	1989-90 to 1993-94		No. of persons employed	1994-95 to 1996-97		No. of persons employed	Growth + or -	
	Total	*Average per year*	*per year (in million)*	*Total*	*Average per year*	*per year (in million*	*Colum 6-3*	*Colum 7-4*
1	2	3	4	5	6	7	8	9
Bangalore rural	52.24	10.44	1.31	34.12	8.53	1.07	-18.30	-18.32
Bangalore urban	105.20	21.40	2.68	60.47	15.11	1.87	-29.39	-30.22
Kolar	198.50	39.70	4.96	101.82	25.45	3.18	-35.89	-35.89
Tumkur	130.44	26.08	3.26	86.78	21.79	2.71	-16.83	-16.87
Chitradurga	1340.22	26.84	3.36	102.50	25.51	3.19	-4.96	-5.06
Shimoga	108.4	21.68	2.71	38.80	9.70	1.21	-55.26	-55.35
Mysore	235.05	47.01	5.88	102.95	25.74	3.22	-45.25	-45.24
Mandya	59.30	11.86	1.48	24.78	6.20	0.77	-47.72	-47.30
Hassan	101.55	20.31	2.54	57.62	14.41	1.80	-29.05	-29.13
Chikmagalur	74.88	14.97	1.87	44.22	11.06	1.38	-26.12	-26.20

(Table Contd....)

(Table 3: Contd...)

(In lakh mandays)

Districts	1989-90 to 1993-94 Total	Average per year	No. of persons employed per year (in million)	1994-95 to 1996-97 Total	Average per year	No. of persons employed per year (in million	Growth + or - Colum 6-3	Colum 7-4
1	2	3	4	5	6	7	8	9
Kodagu	30.92	6.18	0.77	25.52	6.38	0.80	3.24	3.90
Dakshina Kannada	82.31	16.46	2.06	53.18	13.37	1.67	-18.77	-18.93
Belgaum	125.68	25.13	3.14	58.97	14.74	1.84	-41.35	-41.40
Bijapur	176.29	35.25	4.41	86.90	21.73	2.72	-38.35	-38.32
Dharwar	128.39	25.67	3.21	68.44	17.11	2.14	.33.35	-33.33
Uttar Kannada	33.88	6.77	0.85	43.70	10.93	1.37	61.45	61.18
Gulbarga	187.02	37.40	4.67	113.98	28.49	3.56	923.82	-23.77
Raichur	134.08	26.81	3.35	113.85	28.46	3.56	6.15	6.27
Bellary	123.38	24.67	3.08	80.27	20.06	2.51	-18.69	-18.51
Bidar	77.90	15.58	61.62	15.40	1.93	-1.16	-1.02	
All State	2299.63	459.93	57.49	1360.79	340.20	42.53	-26.00	-26.02

Source: Ibid.

up short-term works, less number of mandays of employment, low coverage of poorer sections for JRY works etc. In all the selected villages, the average allocation per village, effective expenditure, mandays of employment created, persons employed under JRY are significantly less as can be seen in table 4. The same is also true in the case of IJRY districts viz., Chitradugra and Tumkur. Furthermore in the case of Chitradurga, although the funds received under JRY is more as compared to other districts, due to more number of villages per panchayat, the same has become thinly scattered at lower level. The effective expenditure in these villages is only Rs. 27,000 and in Hassan district the same is significantly low. This has led to less number of mandays of employment and coverage of persons. Contrary to this, less number of villages covered by each panchayat has its own advantages like more funds availability, more effective expenditure, creating remunerative assets, more number of man-days of employment opportunities etc. In this regard, Dakshin Kannada with higher allocation per village under JRY has generated more employment opportunities for relatively more number of persons. Panchayats in the district have even created revenue yielding assets.

Looking at the asset crated under JRY, if the material and labour charges are bifurcated from the effective expenditure, the amount available for matrial procurement is too small. With the available amount only either spill over works (for completion) or repairs of the existing assets (to upkeep them) would be taken up and not the fresh development work. If at all fresh works are taken up, they could be only a of substandard, very limited and less costly ones. A majority of the panchayats have taken up spill-over works at large scale out of the JRY funds available and eventually to meanest funds viability, the completion of the works has taken long period say 2 to 3 years (table 5). Fresh works which are short term and of less cost includes the construction of drainages, shops, toilets (in the panchayat and in the school), which have been

Table 4: JRY in Selected Villages of Karnataka 1998-99

District	*Taluk*	*Village Pancha-yat covered*	*No. of villges covered*	*Amount received (in lakhs)*	*Alloca-tion village*	*Effec-tive expen-diture per village*	*Mate-rial cost*[2]	*Labour charges*	*Man-day of employ-ment*[3]	*No. of persons emplo-ment*[4]	*No. of days emplo-ment*
Chitradurga	Hiriyur	A	7	2.23	.032	0.25	0.10	0.15	577	72	6
		B	6	2.00	0.33	0.26	0.10	0.16	615	77	9
Tumkur	Gubbi	C	5	1.20	0.24	0.19	0.08	0.11	423	53	6
		D	6	1.37	0.23	0.18	0.07	0.11	423	53	11
Dakshina Kannada	Sulya	E	2	1.71	0.85	0.67	0.27	0.4	1538	192	13
		F	3	1.53	0.51	0.39	0.16	0.23	885	111	9
Hassan	Arasikere	G	9	1.16	0.13	0.10	0.04	0.06	231	29	4
		H	7	1.11	0.16	0.12	0.03	0.09	346	43	7
		Average	5.6	1.54	0.35	0.27	0.11	0.16	630	78	8

Note: 1. After deducting the 22.5 per cent directly benefiting expenditure on SC/ST families.
2. As per the guidelines the expenditure has to be earmarked at 60 : 40 labour charges and material cost respectively.
3. Labour charges divided by the minimum wage rate of Rs. 26 per manday.
4. Total mandays divided by the each manday I.e., 8 hours.
5. Total persons employed divided by the average No. of persons employed (in bracket).

Source: Primary survey through personal visits. In order to maintain secrecy, the names of the villages have been changed.

completed in one year. In the case of the drainages also it is difficult to cover the entire village in one year with the available funds. Inerestingly there are instances to have taken up the drainage as spill-over works in the subsequent years. With least funds, many panchayats have preferred to take up repairs of the road works over any other fresh works. But disheartening fact is that most roads have been washed off in the rains as they were attended only with minor repairs. Further, it goes without mention, wherever high cost works are taken up, they remained incomplete as they could not be completed within the amount released under JRY during that particular financial year. Contrary to this, there are instances of constructing revenue yielding assets with the JRY funds. Commercial buildings and shops were constructed for rental purposes in one of the best considered panchayats, which is getting regular revenue out of the assets created and the same is being spent on village development works in addition to JRY funds.

Table 5: Works completed under JRY in Selected Villages During 1998-99

Panchayats	*Nature of works*	*Name of works*	*Period taken for completion*
A,B,C,D & F	Fresh works	Construction of , drainages shops, toilets and library	Less than a year
A,C,E,F,G & H	Spill-over works	Panchayat offices, school & anganwadi buildings, community, commercial buildings, bridges, entertainment hall etc.	Two to three year
A,C,D, & E	Repair works	Roads	Less than a yaer

Source: Field personal visits.

Other starking realities of JRY are : further fragmentation of resources, lack of funds for asset maintenance, non acceptance of the wages, random selection of beneficiaries/workers etc. Fragmentation of funds across villages falls under village panchayats is the most commonly accepted practice. The same is in vogue as the members answerable to their electoral folk. Otherwise, many members found it difficult to defend themselves. There were instances of considering panchayat members incapable for having not obtained their share of the funds. Members do consult their folks as far as the works to be taken up on the basis of the funds available at their disposal. But in large number of cases works are chosen by the members themselves and entrust these works to contractors of their choice to exeute the same. In either cases, works are taken up with an expenditure of less than Rs. 10,000. Spill over works have been often taken up as and when the cost of fresh works exceeds Rs. 10,000. Generally Zilla panchayats send circular as to how much money is going to be disbursed under JRY and ask gram panchayats to prepare action plan on the basis of the funds availability. Most Gram panchayats have adhered to the circular as there were chances of diversion of funds or stoppage/lapse of the same if it is not adhered to. In a few cases of panchayats such funds have also been consolidated and spent on common benefiting assets and to some extent remunerative assets have also been created to fetch additional revenue. This apart, delay in releasing the JRY funds and releasing grants in instalments have given rise to delay in completion of works and involvement of the contractors involuntarily. Since most gram panchayats have received JRY funds (meagre) in two or three instalments there have been clear understanding between the gram panchayats and the contractors in regard to the continuation of the works. Similarly as contractors executed and supervised the JRY works, they paid the labourers from their own pocket according to their own agreements and they had been paid by the panchayats after receiving money. To our surprise a large number of workers had also been hired from other villages/panchayats by the contractors, for the JRY works at times of need.

Three methods are prevailing for the identification and selection of beneficiaries for JRY works and other benefits. First, random selection of the beneficiaries by the gram panchayat themselves. Labourers have been selected in most cases on the basis of the workers contacts with gram panchayats. In the case of a few panchayats the names of the labourers have been forcefully entered in the nominal muster rolls (NMR) for formalities purposes although they were not employed under JRY works or the works that they were hired for was not necessarily JRY. This means that maintenance of Muster rolls with identified workers available for JRY works has not been followed. Secondly, identification of the beneficiaries by the elected panchayat members themselves especially for the utilisation of 22.5 per cent of funds meant to provide directly benefiting assets to SC/ST poor families. This has been admitted frankly by the members that selection of beneficiaties through grama sabha meeting for these benefits is extremely difficult as it is very hard to convince everyone and that too under the circumstances of meagre availability of funds. It need not be specified again, that followers of the elected panchayat members are the beneficiaries under 22.5 per cent funds and contractors have constructed the dwelling houses as this was opted mostly by the beneficiaries. Final but important is the selection of workers by the contactors. When the works are executed directly by the contractors, panchayats have had hardly any say over them on the selection of workers. But in a good number of instances contractors did hire labourers from other villages/panchayats as they were unable to get the local labourers for the wages they pay. Infact most panchayats have defended their actions, as the same has eliminated supervision of work as well as minimised the embarrassment in payment of lower wages by the panchayats directly.

With regard to the payment of wages, JRY works are found to be unattractive for the labourers as they get much higher wages by the local landlords. Above all, labourers havc preferred to work to the local landlords as they get not only advance wages to meet their contingency expenditure but also regular employment fairly for large number of days. As a result, panchayats under review have experienced hardship in getting labourers and were compelled to pay on par with local wages to carry out JRY works. On an average, unskilled male and female workers had been paid at Rs. 65 and 47.50 respectively, which is two and a half times and around two times higher than the minimum wages or JRY wages of Rs. 26. However for formality purposes, it has been shown by all the panchayats that labourers were paid according to the minimum wages but in reality they were paid in accordance with local wages and book adjustments were done. This is also one of the reasons as to why contractors were involved by the panchayats for the execution of JRY works. This apart, wage discrimination between male and female workers is a perpetual reality under JRY and most panchayats including the workers (especially the women) have agreed to such discrimination. It was admitted that men do strenuous works like digging, cutting etc. and women carrying mud. Since contractor play an important role in executing the JRY, none of them have agreed to pay equal wages for both male and female. Contractors argued frantically for wage discrimination as long as the men does the strenuous works. Surprisingly, in one of the panchayats, female workers were not at all hired as the work taken up was claimed to be too technical. This only further confirms non-adhering to the programme guidelines.

Equally important disarray is lack of up-keeping of the community assets created under JRY, which is very significant from the view point of their services in the long run. At the same time, whenever there is dearth of public investment, maintenance of the community assets assumes greater importance. However, there are hardly any attempts to maintain the JRY assets, as there is no earmarking of funds for the same. In the absence of the same, many of the panchayats have had no funds for asset maintenance (Kripa Shankar, 1994). Although a few panchayats have eatmarked 10 per cent of their developmental funds and few others are maintaining out of their own meagre funds, majority of them have not bothered at all. Many have drawn the resources from other schemes. It has been argued that each panchayat needs anything around Rs.40 to 50,000 per year for maintenance of assets irrespective of under which scheme they were cleared which is a challenging task to mobilise as the revenue sources are limited and irregular on the one hand and meagre developmental receipts on the other hand.

IV

CONCLUSION

Notwithstanding the well-intended objectives of the policies, if adequate financial support is not given, public the purpose of the policy would be defeated. Similarly if such policy failed to reflects the ground realities, the overall impact would be limited. In the case of JRY, not only has there been inadequate financial allocation for its implementation but also the ground realities have impeded the impact. In other words, the overall objectives of creation of community based durable assets and employment generation to the vulnerable groups have been under question. Empirical evidence shows that JRY in Karnataka suffers from a number of weaknesses. One of the major set backs is the large size of the panchayat (which is the unit of implementation of JRY) with more number of villages. In view of this, funds received by the panchayats under JRY fragmented across members of different villages. With this meagre resources, contractors (being the representatives of elected members and panchayats) have executed the less cost oriented works (construction of drainages, toilets, shops, library etc.) which are mostly identified by the members. This type of the works have created only a limited number of employment opportunities to the JRY workers. Also since the funds available for procurement of materials is too small, creation of durable as well as qualitative assets under JRY has not been possible. Therefore, owing to inadequate financial support and fragmentation of public resources, creation of employment opportunities for large number of poor families and development of qualitative and durable assets have been far from reaching objectives. Thus, following are the inferences of the study.

1. The process of employment generation through community based asset creation in rural areas has been significantly impeded with the erosion of public investment under JRY in a large number of districts in Karntaka, during the period between 1994-95 and 1997-98. Especially, there has been a negative growth in investment in half of the identified backward districts in the State. Further as a result of this trend, the net available resources for direct employment generation at the village level is very meagre.

2. Increase in public investment under JRY itself does not bring about the coverage of poorer sections for employment opportunities at large scale and creation of qualitative community based assets. At the same time, fragmentation of investible funds is also associated with low impact of JRY. Evidently, panchayats with less number of villages have not only created more mandays of employment under JRY with more effective investible funds but have also created remunerative assets.

3. Erosion of public investment together with fragmentation of funds have prompted for substantial reduction in the public works and creation of substandard as well as non-durable

assets. In fact in order to utilise the available funds and to complete the incomplete works, left over works have been taken up under JRY. Further, the poor performance of the scheme is also associated with the drop in participation of the poorer sections.

4. Non-acceptance of the JRY works at minimum wages is an indication of the availability of similar works in rural and urban areas at higher market wages. With the increased transportation facilities, wags labourer's mobility and family remittances have also increased. But then this can not be taken as a factor to implement JRY on a lower scale. Since JRY is a unique scheme for community asset creation, its effective implementation in terms of higher allocation and higher wages would go a long way in reducing rural deprivations. This would also facilitate the implementing agencies to minimise the dependency on others i.e., contractor and to provide the benefits to the designated target groups.

To sum up, so long as the employment generation through community assets creation continues as one of the strategies of better quality of life, priority of investment has to be continued on JRY. In addition to priority for higher investment under JRY, alternative methods of funds allocation has to be worked out preferably on the basis of the ground realities. One such alternative could be to take up community based asset creation activities for each village and priorities of works could be worked out on the basis of the funds availability.

Notes

1. Gram Panchayats, the lower tier governments, get 70 per cent of the total funds for implementation

of JRY. The rest is shared between the Zilla and Tuluk Panchayats in the ratio of 15 per cent each.

2. Includes creation of income supplementing assets besides constructing houses for dwelling and open well for irrigating SC/ST lands under Indira Awaas and Million well schemes as they were sub-scheme of JRY.

3. It was a sub-scheme launched in 120 most backward districts in twelve states including 8 districts in Karnataka. 50 per cent of blocks in district under DPAP, high SC/ST population and low agricultural productivity were the germinate factors for assessing district backwardness. This was initiated to evolve special and innovative projects to prevent the immigration of labourers and to enhance the women's employment. Later during 1995 IJRY was merged with Employment Assurance Scheme.

4. It is the net available resources for community asset creation and employment generation after deducting 22.5 per cent from the total towards creating assets directly benefiting SC/ST families.

REFERENCES

1. Raghav Giha (1991), Poverty Alleviation Programmes in Rural India: An Assessment, Development and Change, Vol. 22, pp. 117-54.

2. Vyas V.S. and Pradeep Bhargava (1995), Public Intervention for Poverty Alleviation - An Overview, Economic and Political Weekly, October 14-21, pp. 2559-72.

3. Government of India (1995), Second Concurrent Evaluation of JRY (June 1993-May 1994), Ministry of Rural Areas and Employment, New Delhi.

4. Neelakantan, M. (1993), Jawahar Rozgar Yojana, An Assessment Through Concurrent Evaluation, Economic and Political Weekly, December 3, pp. 3901-97.

5. Neelakantan, M. (1993), Jawahar Rozgar Yojana, An Panchayats and the Poor in India, Asian Survey, Vol. 38, Issue No. 10, pp. 928-49.

6. Parameshwaran Iyer (1994), Creating Rural Employment, JRY New Thrust Areas, Economic and Political Weekly, August 6, pp. 2065-6.

7. Jos Chathukulam and V.K. Kurien (1995), Jawahar Rozgar Yojana: An Assessment, Economic and Political Weekly, February 11, pp. 343-44.

8. Kripa Sirankar (1994), Jawahar Rozgar Yojana: An Assessment in U.P., Economic and Political Weekly, July 16, pp. 1845-8.

10

Role of Women in Dairy Enterprises and Participation in Decision-Making Process:

A Case Study of Smallholder Farms of Uttranchal

*M.L. Sharma, Chandra Dev & B.K. Khanduri**

Introduction

Women contribute significantly in agricultural activities including crop production, horticulture and upkeep of livestock in the hills. Due to lack of employment opportunities in hills most of the male workers migrate to plains in search of jobs and hence, the hill women has to take care of all the farm activities including livestock in addition to their household activities. Almost all the operations pertaining to milk production are performed by women in hills but their participation in decision making process is the least. In most of the cases, decisions are taken by the head of family without consulting the female family members.

Therefore, it is worthwhile to examine the contribution of the women in livestock enterprises through detailed investigation, which will provide valuable informations to the planners, policy makers and researchers for better management of the enterprise. The process of women participation in decision making pertaining to livestock enterprise has its own importance in the effective planning of particular enterprise.Keeping these facts in mind, the present study was conducted in Tehri Garhwal district of Uttranchal with the aims to find out the role of women in dairy enterprise and to workout the extent of participation of women in decision making process related to management and efficient execution of livestock enterprise in the hills.

Methodology

The present study was based on an intensive enquiry of 78 respondents selected from three agro-ecological situations—27 from high-hills (more than 1500 m MSL); 25 from mid-hills (1000-1500m MSL) and 26 from valley (less than 1000m MSL). The district Tehri and block Chamba were selected purposely considering the representative area of Uttranchal in special reference to dairy enterprises. Two villages were selected in each of the three situations. The desired data were collected for one agricultural year 1999-2000. The simple linear regression analysis was used to examine the relationship between contribution of male and female workers and yield of the milk. The same analysis was made for participation of women in decision-making and yield of the milk. The linear regression equation is as follows:

$$Y = a + b_1x_1 + b_2x_2$$

Where, Y = Yield of milk/farm/year in Kg;

X = contribution of male and female on milk production in days/farm/year or Participation of male and female in decision making in percentage;

a = Intercept

b = Regression coefficient;

Result and Discussion

In a farm-family, on an average, total number of family members were 8.26 persons out of that about 44 per cent were agricultural workers and 17 per cent non-agricultural. The migrants were about 20 per cent. The average number of milch animal was 1.36 animals/farm which varied from 1.28 in mid hills to 1.47 in high hills. Buffalo and cow were main source of milk production in the hilly farms. Most of the farmers preferred to maintain buffalo for milk production whereas few cows were also kept for this purpose. Out of the total farm animals, about 60 per cent were milch animals.

Table 1: Average number of animals maintained on the sample farms

(Animals/farm)

Animals	*Valley*	*Mid-hill*	*High-hill*	*Overall*
Buffalo	1.34	1.24	1.44	1.34
Cow	—	0.04	0.03	0.02
Young stock	0.42	0.60	0.29	0.43
Bullock	0.96	0.48	0.07	0.50
Total	2.72	2.36	1.83	2.29

The employment pattern of human labor for upkeep of milch animals is presented in Table 2, which reveals that on an average total number of human labour required for upkeep of the animals was 149.06 days per animal out of which only 10 per cent were devoted by male and remaining 90 per cent by female members. These results clearly indicate that most of the livestock operations were performed by female members. On an average 133-98 days per animal were spent by women on upkeep of milch animals in a year. The lion's share of total human labour was on fodder collection being 57.66% of the total human labour days followed by cleaning of cattle shed 13.55% days. Out of 83.74% days spent for fodder collection by the women, about 96 per cent were on green fodder and 4 per cent on dry fodder collection. It is interesting to note that about 67 per cent women labor was used for fodder collection from the forest and 33 per cent from owned field. As the common practice, no fodder crop was grown on cultivated fields. Fetching of water and milking and preparation of milk products required about 15 days each per animal/year. The Table 2 further revealed that contribution of male to the milk production was limited to the marketing of milk and that of milk products only, which accounted for about 59 per cent of the total labour contributed by male membes. The altitude-wise employment pattern revealed that the highest contribution made by women to milk production was on high hills being 176.22 days/animal/year and least on the mid hills where women contributed 110.6 days. The highest contribution of male was in mid hills (22.86 days). Out of the total human labour required for milk production in valleys more than 92 per cent was shared by women and remaining 8 per cent by men. In the mid hills, about 83 per cent labour was contributed by female workers whereas in high hills it was about 94 per cent.

The results showed that the highest labour required for fodder collection was on high hills and the lowest in mid hills. The availability of fodder in vicinity of mid hills was sufficient whereas acute shortage of fodder was in high hills. The operation wise break up portrayed that contribution of women for fodder collection was 65 per cent in valleys, 63 per cent in mid hills and about 60 per cent of the total women labour in high hills. In the cleaning of cattle shed, about 95 per cent contribution was made by women in valleys, 92 per cent in mid hills and 100 per cent in high hills. In fetching of water for milch animals, about 96 per cent labour contribution was made by women in valleys, 85 per cent in mid hills and 94 per cent in high hills. The milking and preparation of milk products indicated the similar trend as it was in case of fodder collection. In this operation the contribution of women ranged from about 20 days/animal/year in high hills to 11 days/animal/year in valley situation. These results clearly indicate that the fodder collection, fetching of water, cleaning of cattleshed and milking operation were almost the sole responsibility of women in the area. The contribution made by male family members

Table 2: Employment of human labour for up keeps of milch animals in Uttranchal.

(Day/animal/year)

Operations	*Valley*		*Mid-hill*		*High-hill*		*Average*		*Total*
	Male	*Female*	*Male*	*Female*	*Male*	*Female*	*Male*	*Female*	
1. Fodder collection									
a. Green fodder from owned field	0.30	28.27	0.00	16.00	1.82	35.05	0.62 (2.30)	26.30 (97.70)	26.92 (100.00)
b. Green fodder from forest	2.60	49.20	0.00	51.00	2.01	66.17	1.58 (2.81)	54.50 (97.19)	56.08 (100.00)
c. Dry fodder	0.00	2.00	0.00	2.30	0.00	5.04	0.00 (0.00)	2.94 (100.00)	2.94 (100.00)
2. Fetching of water	0.50	14.10	1.40	7.90	1.36	20.52	1.03 (6.92)	13.85 (93.08)	14.88 (100.00)
3. Cleaning of cattle shed	0.90	16.70	1.60	17.20	0.00	25.58	0.87 (4.30)	19.33 (95.70)	20.20 (100.00)
4. Milking & preparation of milk products	0.40	11.00	0.30	15.70	0.00	19.86	0.25 (1.63)	15.00 (98.37)	15.25 (100.00)
5. Marketing of milk and milk	3.20	2.00	19.50	0.50	4.74	0.36	8.97 (89.52)	1.05 (10.48)	10.02 (100.00)
6. Miscellaneous	2.80	0.00	0.06	0.00	2.32	3.64	1.76 (63.53)	1.01 (36.47)	2.77 (100.00)
Total (7.96)	10.70 (7.96)	123.70 (92.04)	22.96 (17.12)	110.60 (82.88)	12.25 (6.49)	176.22 (93.51)	15.08 (10.11)	133.98 (89.89)	149.06 (100.00)

Figures in parentheses are the percentage values.

was less than 5 per cent except for fetching of water in mid hills where about 15 per cent work was shared by male members.

The results revealed that marketing of milk and milk products were almost in the hands of male family members in which on an aveage, men spent about 9 days/animal/ year. The contribution of women was the highest in valleys, on marketing of milk and milk products being 2 days/ animal/year but in high and mid hills female contribution was almost negligible for this operation. The contribution of male on marketing operation was the highest min mid hills because of the fact that there was much more marketed surplus of milk in this situation as compared to high hills and valleys. The contribution made by male on marketing of milk was about 20 days in mid hills, 5 days in high hills and 3 days/animals/year in valleys.

The contribution of male and female workers for the upkeep of milch animals on per farm basis is given in Table 3. The table 3 depicts that on an average about 198 days labour was required for fodder collection on a farm. Out of this, 193 days were contributed by female and remaining 5 days by male members. The cleaning of cattleshed and milking of milch animals accounted for about 47 days and 35 days/farm/year, respectively and out of that a loin's share was contributed by female family members. The overall average revealed that about 352 days per farm human labour was required to upkeep of the milch animals out of that 309 days devoted by female and 43 days by male members. The altitude wise employment of labour indicated that highest contribution of female for milk production was on valley farms being about 338 days/farm/year followed by high hills (326 days) whereas it was comparatively low in mid hill situation where 261 days female labour was required. Under valley condition, about 64.59 per cent of the total women labour was spent for fodder collection, 13.5 per

Table 3: Employment of human labour for up keeps of milch animals in Uttranchal.

(Days/farm/year)

Operations	Valley		Mid hill		High-hill		Average		Total
	Male	Female	Male	Female	Male	Female	Male	Female	
1. Fodder collection									
a. Green fodder from owned field	0.81 (2.77)	78.37 (23.20)	0.00 —	37.76 14.47	3.37 (14.87)	64.90 (19.89)	1.43 (3.35)	60.69 (19.63)	62.12 (17.65)
b. Green fodder	7.10 (24.33)	134.35 (39.77)	0.00 —	120.36 (46.12)	3.72 (16.42)	122.53 (37.55)	3.64 (8.53)	125.76 (40.68)	129.40 (36.78)
c. Dry fodder	0.00 —	5.46 (1.62)	0.00 —	5.42 (2.07)	0.00 —	9.33 (2.86)	0.00 —	6.78 (2.19)	6.78 (1.93)
2. Fetching of water	1.36 (4.66)	38.50 (11.40)	3.30 (6.12)	18.64 (7.14)	2.51 (11.08)	38.00 (11.65)	2.37 (5.55)	31.96 (10.34)	34.33 (9.76)
3. Cleaning of cattle shed	2.45 (8.40)	45.60 (13.50)	3.77 (6.99)	40.59 (15.55)	0.00 —	47.37 (14.52)	2.02 (4073)	44.60 (14.43)	46.62 (13.25)
4. Milking & preparation of milk products	1.09 (3.74)	30.03 (8.89)	0.70 (1.30)	37.05 (14.20)	0.00 —	36.77 (11.27)	0.58 (1.36)	34.61 (11.20)	35.19 (10.00)
5. Marketing of milk and milk products	8.73 (29.92)	5.46 (1.62)	46.02 (85.33)	1.18 (0.45)	8.77 (38.70)	0.66 (0.20)	20.69 (48.48)	2.42 (0.78)	23.11 (6.57)
6. Miscellaneous	7.64 (26.18)	0.00 —	0.14 (0.26)	0.00 —	4.29 (18.93)	6.74 (2.06)	11.95 (28.00)	2.32 (0.75)	14.27 (4.06)
Total	29.18 (100)	337.77 (100)	53.93 (100)	261.00 (100)	22.66 (100)	326.30 (100)	42.68 (100)	309.14 (100)	351.82 (100)

Figures in Parentheses are the percentage values.

cent on cleaning of cattleshed and 11.4 per cent of fetching of water for animals. Milking and preparation of milk products accounted for 8.89 per cent for total women days employed in the situation whereas marketing of milk needed least involvement of women as there was only 1.62 per cent of the total women days in the operation. In marketing of milk and milk products the highest percentage of male labour was required being about 30 per cent of the total male labour employed in valley situation. The second important operation was miscellaneous in which 26.18 per cent of total male labour were involved. The miscellaneous operation included insemination of animals, veterinary assistance etc. In mid hill situation, about 63 per cent of the total female working days were involved on fodder collection and 15.55 per cent on cleaning of cattleshed. The milking and preparation of milk products needed 14.2 per cent and fetching of water for animals 7.14 per cent of the total women days employed in mid hills for milk production. The contribution of male family members was the highest for marketing being 46 days/farm/year in mid hills. It was mainly due to more marketed surplus in the mid hill situation. Out of 326 days/farm/year women contribution to milk production, abut 197 days was on fodder collection, 47 days on cleaning of cattle-shed and 38 days in fetching of water on high hills. The milking and preparation of milk products required about 37 days/farm/year women labour in mid-hills whereas the miscellaneous activities consumed nearly 7 days/farm/year female labour. Out of 23 days male labour employed on milk production in high hills, the highest percentage was on marketing of milk followed by miscellaneous operations. These findings give a clear-cut understanding that the womenfolk contribute very remarkable amount of labour for milk production in all the three agro-ecological situations. The male contribution was significant only for marketing operation of milk and milk products.

The participation of women in decision-making process is a very crucial and important for livestock enterprises in the hills because most of livestock operations were performed by the women. Hence, it would be appropriate that a person who is performing most of operations must take part in the managerial and decision making process. The participation of women in decision-making relating to dairy enterprises on the sample farms of Uttranchal is given in Table 4. It is evident from the Table 4 that 29 per cent decisions were taken by women and 33 per cent by male family members in the valleys whereas 38 per cent decisions were taken jointly by male and female both. In case of mid hills, 20 per cent decisions taken by female alone and 42 per cent by male without consulting the female family members. In high hills, 35 per cent cases were decided by female memebrs and 23 per cent by male members. The altitude wise analysis of participation of women revealed that the highest participation of women was in disposal of young stock in all the three altitudes ranging from 39 per cent in valley to 56 per cent in mid hills. The second important matter in which the woman participated extensively was decision regarding insemination of the animals. It was mainly due to the fact that the female family members were closely associated with upkeep of milch animals particularly during lactation period.

The decisions related with hiring-in and hiring-out of the labour were extensively handled by male family members in valleys and mid hills. Most of the decisions related to selection of breed of the animals and number of animals to be maintained on the farm were taken jointly by both in the valleys, 40 pre cent by male and 24 pre cent by female in mid hill and 26 per cent by male and 33 pre cent by female in high hills. The purchase and sale of animals was decided by male family member in valley and mid hills whereas almost jointly by both in high hills.In veterinary related

Table 4: Participation of women in decision-making on the matters related to dairy enterprises.

Particulars	Valley				Mid-hill				High-hill			
	Male	*Female*	*M + F*	*Total*	*Male*	*Female*	*M + F*	*Total*	*Male*	*Female*	*M + F*	*Total*
1. Types & number of Animal	1 (4.0)	6 (23.0)	19 (73.0)	26 (40.0)	10 (24.0)	6 (36.0)	9 (100)	25 (26.0)	7 (33.0)	9 (41.0)	11 (100)	27
2. Purchase & sale of animal	12 (46.0)	3 (12.0)	11 (42.0)	26 (100)	13 (52.0)	3 (12.0)	9 (36.0)	25 (100)	7 (26.0)	7 (26.0)	13 (48.0)	27 (100)
3. Veterinary related decision	13 (54.0)	8 (33.0)	3 (13.0)	24 (100)	13 (52.0)	9 (36.0)	3 (12.0)	25 (100)	9 (33.0)	10 (37.0)	8 (30.0)	27 (100)
4. Hiring of the labour	15 (68.0)	4 (18.0)	3 (14.0)	22 (100)	14 (74.0)	2 (10.0)	3 (16.0)	19 (100)	11 (41.0)	7 (26.0)	9 (33.0)	27 (100)
5. Sale of milk and milk products	3 (18.0)	6 (35.0)	8 (47.0)	17 (100)	4 (17.0)	9 (39.0)	10 (44.0)	23 (100)	3 (14.0)	6 (27.0)	13 (59.0)	22 (100)
6. Disposal of young stock	4 (15.0)	10 (39.0)	12 (46.0)	26 (100)	4 (56.0)	14 (28.0)	7 (100)	25 (7.0)	2 (52.0)	14 (41.0)	11 (100)	27
7. Decision regarding insemination of animals	6 (23.0)	10 (39.0)	10 (38.0)	26 (100)	10 (40.0)	5 (20.0)	10 (40.0)	25 (100)	6 (22.0)	10 (37.0)	11 (41.0)	27 (100)
Overall average	8 (33.0)	7 (29.0)	9 (38.0)	24 (100)	10 (42.0)	7 (29.0)	7 (29.0)	24 (100)	6 (23.0)	9 (35.0)	11 (42.0)	26 (100)

Figures in parentheses are the percentage values.

decisions male opinion was dominated in valleys and mid hills whereas equal importance was given to both the members in high hills.The sale of milk and milk products related decisions taken by both the family members in all the three situations and women showed a slightly higher participation in these decisions.Thus,we can conclude from these results that there was no certain trend regarding participation of male and female family members in the livestock enterprises. Although the work-load showed by women was extraordinary higher in all the three agro-ecological situations but in decision making process women were excluded traditionally to a great extent therefore, it is an urgent need to increase the participation of women in the decision making process at the existing pattern of milk production in the hills.

Regression Analysis for Contribution/Participation of Women in Decision-making and Milk Production

The simple linear regression analysis was made for contribution of women in milk production and their participation in decision-making process considering milk yield as a dependent variable. The results of analysis are presented in Table 5. It is evident from the Table that the R^2 for all the equations indicated significant values adopted for contribution made by male and female workers for milk production in high hills, mid hills and valley situations except for male in high hills. The R^2 values indicated 15.66 per cent variation in the milk yield due to variation in the contribution of female workers in valleys, 20.79 per cent in mid hills and 26.36 per cent variation in high hills. The regression coefficient showed positive significant values for all the equations except for male for high hills. It refelcts that the impact of female workers was remarkable in all the situation on milk production in the hills whereas in high hill situation, regression coefficient of female was 3.78 proving remarkable impact of female labour on milk production. The non-significant regression coefficient of male in high hills portrarys that female has no impact on milk production in high hill situation.

Table 5: Results of regression Analysis Made for Contribution of Male and Female Workers and Milk Production.

Variable (X)	*Intercept* (a)	*Regression coefficient* (b)	*Standard Error* (SE)	*Coefficient of determination* (R^2)
Valleys				
Male (days/farm)	1491.15	5.50*	2.20	0.2137*
Female (days/farm)	1051.31	2.12*	1.03	0.1566*
Mid-hill				
Male (days/farm)	1626.49	6.79*	2.17	0.2993*
Female (days/farm)	1103.23	3.33*	1.36	0.2079*
High-hill				
Male (days/farm)	1919.39	-6.72	4.75	0.0741
Female (days/farm)	531.28	3.78*	1.26	0.2636*

The regression analysis made for estimating that relationship between decision-making process by male and female workers relating to the dairy matters and milk production on the farms. The results are presented in Table 6. The table 6 portrays that all the equations indicated non-significant values of R^2 except for female worker in the high hill situation where it was significant at 5 per cent level of significance and showing 18.93 per cent variation in the milk production due to variation in the decision making process of the women workers. The significant values of regression coefficient indicating statistically remarkable impact of women in decision making on the dairy enterprises at high hill situations.

Table 6: Result of Regression Analysis Made for Participation in Decision Making and Yield of Milk

Variable (X)	*Intercept* (a)	*Regression coefficient* (b)	*Standard Error* (SE)	*Coefficient of determination* (R^2)
Valley				
Male (days/farm)	1500.74	73.54	70.92	0.0447
Female (days/farm)	1548.55	59.07	81.76	0.0221
Mid-hill				
Male (days/farm)	2059.94	-24.09	61.04	0.0067
Female (days/farm)	2014.85	-10.65	59.57	0.0010
High-hill				
Male (days/farm)	1971.06	-11.91	6.12	0.1363
Female (days/farm)	1352.63	9.57*	4.04	0.1893*

Conclusions

The results of the study establish the fact that the contribution of women was significant and remarkable to milk production in all the three agro-ecological situations of Uttranchal. The participation of women in decision-making proved that only the female workers had statistically significant impact on milk production under high hill situation at the existing pattern of milk production in smallholder farms of Uttranchal.

REFERENCES

1. Puri, Shashi (1972). Rural families and decision-making pattern. *Indian Journal of Extension Education,* 7(1-2), 65-67.

2. Singh, D.V. and Bhati, J.P. (1985). Women in hill agriculture. A case study of Himachal Pradesh (Summary). *Indian Journal of Agricultural Economics,* 40 (3), 269.

3. Sisodia, J.S. (1985), Role of farm women in agriculture. A study of Chambal Comnmand Area of Madhya Pradesh. *Indian Journal of Agricultural Economics,* 40 (3), 223-230.

4. Tripathi, R.S. (1995). Level and pattern of female labour in the production of hill crops of central Himalaya. *Journal of Hill Research,* Sikkim Science Society, 8 (1), 9-18.

5. Tripathi, R.S. (1999). Inadequate participation of hill farm women in decision making-A gender constraint analysis. *Proceedings of the seventh Annual Conference of Agricultural Economics Research Association (India),* New Delhi held on Oct. 6-7 at Dharwad (Karnataka).

6. Verma, J.C. (1978). Women in rural economy. *Kurukshetra,* 26 (11), 7-10.

6

Participation of Rural Women in Livestock Production System in Uttar Pradesh (India)

Raj Kishor, G.N. Singh & D.S. Singh

Introduction

India is endowed with significant share of the world's livestock population. It's livestock sector has started showing a significant impact on the growth of the country's economy. Its share in agriculture Gross Domestic Product (GDP) has risen from 17 per cent in 1980-81 to 26 per cent in 1996-97. It is the principal source of draft power in rural areas which provides milk, meat, eggs, wool, hides and spins, manure and fuel. This sector continues to demonstrate a beneficial impact on about 50 crores rural poor by improving their income, employment and consumption pattern and thereby act as a potential tool in alleviating rural poverty. Rural women play a significant role in domestic and social economic life of the country, and therefore, national development is not possible without development of this important and substantial segment of the society. From times immemorial women have played a vital role in livestock production system. In addition to the livestock production activities considerable part of rural women's time was spent in different activities related to livestock production system. They were found to be mainly responsible for care of animals and they were actively participate in all the activities related to livestock production system. Although rural women belonging to all the categories of land holdings participating in some extent in activities related to livestock production, but women belonging to specially marginal and small categories of land holdings to a large extent participate in livestock production than the others (medium and large land holdings). Thus the present study focused only these two categories of land holdings. The participation of rural women in various tasks related to livestock production and their times spent in the work may be affected by many factors. In some cases male members of family or servants do these activities. Some rural women also provide their services to outside, generally of lower castes, especially in making cow dung cakes, and manure, cleaning cattle shed and grazing animals.

Many researchers have not explored role of rural women in livestock production system in Uttar Pradesh. Thus, considering the importance of rural women in livestock production system, the present study was conducted in district Sitapur of Central Region of Uttar Pradesh during the year 1998-99. To examine the role of rural women in livestock production system and time spent in the same, 10 activities related to livestock production were identified for the present study, keeping in mind their importance for the same. Time spent by rural women in various tasks of livestock production was affected by a number of factors i.e. age, education, type of family, size of holding, caste and socio-economic status of respondents in both area and categories separately these were also explored in this study.

Objectives

The main objectives of the study were

1. To examine the pattern of rural women performing activities related to livestock production system.

2. To work out time spent by rural women in various activities related to livestock production under different areas and size of holdings.

3. To study the factors affecting their participation and time spent in livestock production system.

Research Methodology

For the purpose of the present study, a multi-stage stratified random sampling procedure was adopted for the selection of district, blocks, villages and households from the Central Region of U.P. In the first stage, only one district namely Sitapur was selected randomly from Central Region of U.P. In the second stage, a sample of two development blocks namely, Khairabad and Sidhauli were selected at random from 19 development blocks of their district. The villages of the selected development blocks were categorized into two i.e. nearer to city/urban areas and interior/remote areas. Villages nearer to city areas were well connected to pucca road/railways and situated to less than 10 Km to urban/city areas. Whereas villages to remote areas/interior areas included to those villages who were situated to adjoining Sitapur City and Sidhauly is situated nearer to Lucknow City. Both the selected blocks were progressive in livestock production. In the third stage, 16 villages (4 from nearer to city areas and 4 from remote areas of each development block), were selected at random. Selected villages were then categorized into two, i.e. nearer to the city areas and interior/remote areas. A list of all households having at least one milch animal (falling near city and interior areas) of selected villages in both the blocks was prepared. Households were further categorized into two, i.e. marginal and small size of land holdings. In the last stage, 200 households were selected randomly (50 from each area of each block i.e. 100 from each block) from 16 villages on the basis of probability proportion to their size of holding and number of households falling under each category and villages. The data were collected by survey method from all the respondents who were personally interviewed with the help of pre-prepared structured schedule.

Results and Discussion

Socio-economic Structure of Sample Households

The data related to sample size, family size, number of worker, caste status, average size of land holding educational level and family type of respondents are summarized in Table 1.

Table 1: Socio-economic Structure of Sample Households

S. No. particulars	Categories of households (in ha.)				Total
	Near to city areas		Interior areas		
	Marginal	Small	Marginal	Small	
1. Sample size of household**	60 (30.00)	40 (20.00)	54 (27.00)	46 (23.00)	200 (100.00)
2. Family size of household*	263 (4.38)	191 (4.78)	272 (5.04)	237 (5.75)	963 (4.82)
a. Male*	134 (2.23)	98 (2.45)	38 (2.56)	120 (2.61)	490 (2.45)
b. Female*	129 (2.15)	93 (2.33)	134 (2.48)	117 (2.54)	473 (2.37)
3. No. of worker*	174 (2.90)	125 (3.13)	175 (324)	155 (3.37)	629 (3.15)
a. male*	89 (1.48)	64 (1.60)	90 (1.67)	80 (1.74)	323 (1.62)
b. female*	85 (1.42)	61 (1.53)	85 (1.57)	75 (1.63)	306 (1.53)
4. caste status**					
a. lower**	14 (23.33)	10 (25.00)	18 (33.33)	12 (26.09)	54 (27.00)
b. middle**	27 (45.00)	18 (45.00)	28 (51.85)	24 (52.17)	97 (48.50)
c. upper**	19 (31.67)	12 (30.00)	8 (14.82)	10 (21.74)	49 (24.50)
5. average size of holding	0.78	1.42	0.84	1.72	1.14

6. type of livestok on sample households *					
a. cattle"	95 (1.58)	72 (1.80)	114 (2.11)	86 (1.87)	367 (1.84)
b. buffaloes *	35 (0.58)	36 (0.90)	78 (1.44)	70 (1.52)	219 (1.10)
c. sheep*	15 (0.25)	8 (0.20)	28 (0.52)	17 (0.37)	68 (0.34)
d. goats*	25 (0.42)	17 (0.43)	74 (1.37)	55 (1.20)	171 (0.86)
e. poultry*	78 (1.30)	54 (1.35)	132 (2.44)	96 (2.09)	360 (1.80)
f. Total livestock (excluding poultry)*	170 (2.83)	133 (3..33)	324 (6.00)	228 (4.96)	825 (4.13)
7. Educational level of respondents*					
a. Illiterate**	36 (60.00)	20 (50.00)	39 (72.22)	29 (63.04)	124 (62.00)
b. Up-to primary**	19 (31.67)	11 (27.50)	12 (22.22)	10 (21.74)	52 (26.00)
c. Middle**	3 (5.00)	5 (12.50)	2 (3.71)	4 (8.70)	14 (7.00)
d. Above middle**	2 (3.33)	4 (10.00)	1 (1.85)	3 (6.52)	10 (5.00)
8. Family type**					
a. Nuclear**	35 (58.33)	22 (55.00)	22 (40.74)	13 (28.26)	92 (46.00)
b. Jont**	25 (41.67)	18 (45.00)	32 (59.26)	33 (71.74)	108 (54.00)

* Figurers in parentheses indicate their average per household.

** Figures in prentheses indicate their percentage of their total

Data depicted Table 1. shows that average sizes of land holding were 1.14 hectare, it was 0.78 hectare, it was 0.78 and 1.42 hectare on marginal and small holdings in nearer city areas and 0.84 and 1.72 hectare on marginal and small holdings in remote areas. Average size of livestock per household in nearer city areas were 2.83 and 3.33 animals on marginal and small size of holdings in nearer city areas and 6.00 and 4.96 animals on the categories in remote areas, respectively. Most of the respondents were illiterate (62.00 per cent) and its percentage was lower in small categories of both areas than marginal. This calls sound policy for improvement for educational level of women in the rural areas. Rural women belonging to nuclear family, participating more in livestock production than joint family in nearer cities area and vice-versa in the remote areas.

Pattern of Participation of Rural Women in Livestock Production

Women were found to be mainly responsible for care of animals and they were participating in all the activities related to livestock production. In very few cases males and servants did these. The data regarding pattern of performing activities related to livestock production in the selected household are presented in Table 2. From the analysis of the patter of performing activities related to livestock production, it was found that on an average in 65 per cent households women alone were performing all the activities related to livestock production without any help from their male members or servants. Followed by 15.50 per cent household's women shared these activities with males of the family, in 5.00 per cent with servants an in 5.00 per cent with both male members of the family and servants. Thus, in 90.50 per cent household's women were participating in the activities related to livestock production. Against it only in 4.00 per cent households these activities were done by males of the family alone, in 3.50 per cent household's males shared with servants and in 2.00 per cent households it was done by servants alone.

As regard area wise and farm category wise break-up of pattern of performing activities related to livestock production indicates that adjoining area to city, 89.00 per cent women of both marginal and small holding households were participating in activities related to livestock production.

Table 2: Pattern of performing activities related to livestock production on sample households

S. No.	Activities performer	Nearer/adjoining city areas		Interior remote areas		Total
		Marginal holding	Small holding	Marginal holding	Small holding	
1.	Women alone	40	22	38	30	130
		(66.67)	(55.00)	(70.37)	(65.21)	(65.00)
2.	Women and male	09	07	08	07	31
		(15.00)	(17.50)	(14.81)	(15.21)	(15.50)
3.	Servant and women	.3	.3	.2	.2	10
		(5.00)	(7.50)	(3.70)	(4.34)	(5.00)
4.	Servant, Women and male of family	02	03	03	02	10
		(3.33)	(7.50)	(5.56)	(4.35)	(5.00)
5.	Male alone	02	01	02	01	07
		(3.33)	(2.50)	(3.70)	(6.52)	(4.00)
6.	Male and Servants	03	02	02	02	07
		(5.00)	(5.00)	(1.85)	(2.17)	(3.50)
7.	Servants	01	02	—	01	04
		(1.67)	(5.00)	—	(2.17)	(2.00)
	Total	60	40	54	46	200
		(30.00)	(20.00)	(27.00)	(23.00)	(100.00)
	Rate of women participation	54	35	51	41	181
		(90.00)	(87.50)	(94.44)	(89.13)	(90.50)

Figure in parentheses show their percentages to total

Whereas, it was about 92.00 per cent in interior/remote areas of district. According to land holdings of households, participation of women in task related to livestock production was highest being 94.44 per cent in marginal holding of interior areas and 90.00 per cent in city adjoining areas of district in same category. In case of small land holding, participation of women was 89.11 per cent in interior areas and 87.50 per cent in city adjoining areas. It is further noted that all the activities related to livestock production were done by women alone without any help from males and servants was highest being 70.37 and 66.67 per cent on marginal land holdings of interior areas and city adjoining areas, respectively. Whereas it was 65.21 per cent and 55.00 per cent in case of small land holding of interior areas and city adjoining areas, respectively. The data related to area wise and categories wise average time spent by owmne in different activities related to livestock production are summarized in Table. 3.

The data of table 3 reveals that on an average total time spent by women in different activities of livestock production was 144.52 minutes (2.41 hours/day) per day. Of which highest amount of time was spent in carrying fodder from his own field, others fields as well as from pasture land/ forest, followed by care of animals including bathing and cleaning of animals, making cow dung cakes, grazing animals, feeding fodder, giving drinking water, making cow dung manure, chaff cutting and milking received 24.60, 14.79, 12.83, 12.30, 12.21, 10.65, 9.65 and 7.94 minutes daily, respectively. Rest activities needs only 8.22 minutes daily. In all these activities of livestock production, highest amount of time 88.86 minutes (3.14 hour) was spent on marginal land holding category farms of interior areas and 163.30 minutes (2.72 hour) on small land holding farms in same area. In case of adjoining city area highest amout of time .(124.90 minutes) was spent by marginal land holding women and 101.05 minutes time spent by small land holdings. Among all the activities related to livestock production, the average time spent in carrying of fodder was highest in all the category and care as of households, due to poor availability, of fodder in comparison to their demand. As regards total time spent in all the activities of livestock production in interior areas was higher in comparison to city adjoining areas. It is further

Table 3: Time spent by women in activities related to livestock production

(minutes/women/day)

S.No.	Activity	*Nearer/ Adjoining city areas*		*Interior/ remote aeas*		*Average*
		Size of holdings		*Size of holdings*		
		Marginal	*Small*	*Marginal*	*Small*	
1.	Care of animals	22.50	18.20	30.50	27.20	24.60
2.	Carrying fodder	25.20	22.40	42.20	35.50	31.33
3.	Chaff cutting	6.25	6.50	15.60	10.25	9.65
4.	Feeding fodder	12.50	10.80	13.25	12.40	12.30
5.	Grazing animals	7.20	5.10	21.50	17.50	12.83
6.	Giving drinking water	11.50	10.50	14.25	12.60	12.21
7.	Cleaning cattle-shed	3.25	2.50	4.55	4.10	3.60
8.	Milking	6.75	5.25	9.50	10.25	7.94
9.	Making cow dung manure	10.50	8.20	12.50	11.40	10.65
10.	Making dung cakes	15.40	8.80	18.75	16.20	14.79
11.	Selling milk	2.20	1.60	4.54	4.05	3.10
12.	Others	1.55	1.20	1.72	1.60	1.52
	Total time	124.90	101.05	188.86	163.30	144.52
		(2.08)	(1.68)	(3.14)	(2.72)	(2.41)

Figures in parentheses indicate time in hours.

noted that women of small categories of both areas devoting less time in activities related livestock production than marginal categories. This may be due the reason that women's of small category help received from servants on one hand and on the other dairying had been adopted as subsidiary occupation in many cases, thereby transferring many of the activities to males whom performed it on commercial basis.

Factors Affecting Participation of women and Time Spent in Livestock Production

The participation of rural women in different activities related to livestock production and its extent depend on various factors. In this regards Table 4 shows that respondent belonging middle (21-35 years) and upper middle (36-50 years) age groups participated more than lower and upper age groups. Similar age groups also spending more time i.e. more 2.0 hours per day in livestock production followed by lower and upper age groups. 10-20 respondents reported that they did not regularly devoting time in livestock production. Percentage of respondent who spending more than 2.0 hours were highest in nuclear family (27.17 per cent), whereas in case of joint family it were only 17.44 per cent. Majority of the respondent of both types family spending 1-2 hours time per day.

Education is another important factor related to livestock production. Respondents belonging to illiterate, participated highest being 62 per cent, followed by up-to primary, middle and upper middle at 26.00, 7.00 and 5.00 per cent, respectively. This shows that participation of women in livestock production activities decreases with the increase in level of education. It was found that more than 2 hours and 1-2 hour's time daily spending by women in livestock production decreases with the increase in level of education of respondents. Against it time spending up to 1 hours and sometime participation of respondent's increases with the increase in level of education. It is noted that more educated spent less time in livestock production, due to reason of that they offer more time in other domestic activities. As regards caste status, respondents of middle castes participation was highest being 48.50 per cent, followed by lower and upper caste respondents, came to 27.00 and 24.50 per cent, respectively. Whereas higher percentage of respondents spending more than 2 hours time, belonging lower caste (31.48 per cent), followed by middle

(20.62 per cent) and upper castes (9.28 per cent). Respondents belonging to upper castes werefound spending less time in livestock production than middle and lower castes. Similar trends were noticed in case of socio-economic status of respondents. Respondents belonging to middle socio-economic status were participating highest being 59.00 per cent, followed by lower (22.50 per cent) and upper castes (18.50 per cent). Respondents belonging to low socio-economic status, spending more time (1-2) hours and 2 hours) in livestock production than others. Amount of time devoted by women in livestock production system decreases with the rising level of socio-economic status of respondent.

Conclusions

It is concluded from the present study that on an average in 65 per cent households women alone were performing all the activities related to livestock production without any help from their male members or servants. It is further noted that women of small categories of both areas devoting less time in activities related to livestock production than marginal categories. Among different activities related to livestock production and time devoted by them is given in descending order, highest amount of time was spent in carrying fodder from his own field, others fields as well as from pasture land/forest, followed by care of animals including bathing and cleaning of animals, making cow dung cakes, grazing animals, feeding fodder, giving drinking water, making cow dung manure, chaff cutting and milking. Among all the activities related to livestock production, the average time spent in carrying of fodder was highest in all the category and areas of households, due to poor availability of fodder in comparison to their demand. As regards total time spent in all the activities of livestock production in interior area was higher in comparison to city adjoining areas, due to higher size of livestock holding in interior areas than nearer city areas. It is further noted that women of small categories of both areas devoting less time in activities

Table 4: Factors affecting participation of women and time spend in livestock production

S. No. Factors	Daily time devoted by women (in hours)				Total
	Sometime	Up to 1	1-2	>2	
A. Age of respondents (Years)					
Upto 20	2	4	4	3	13
	(15.38)	(30.77)	(30.77)	(23.08)	(6.50)
21-35	10	12	31	34	87
	(11.49)	(13.79)	(35.63)	(39.08)	(43.50)
36-50	8	18	30	24	80
	(10.00)	(22.50)	(37.50)	(30.00)	(40.00)
Above 50	4	5	8	3	20
	(20.00)	(25.00)	(40.00)	(15.00)	(10.00)
B. Family type of respondents					
Nuclear	10	21	36	25	92
(10.92)	(22.83)	(39.13)	(27.17)	(46.00)	
Jonit	25	27	48	18	108
	(13.89)	(25.00)	(44.44)	(16.67)	(54.00)
C. size of land holding of respondents					
Marginal	16	32	50	26	114
	(14.04)	(28.07)	(43.86)	(22.81)	(57.00)
Small	9	28	36	15	86
	(10.67)	(32.56)	(41.86)	(17.44)	(43.00)
D. Education of respondents					
Illiterate	14	24	60	26	0124
	(11.29)	(19.35)	(48.39)	(20.97)	(62.00)
Up to primary	6	15	21	10	52
	(11.54)	(28.85)	(40.35)	(19.23)	(26.00)
Middle	3	7	3	2	14
	(21.42)	(42.86)	(21.42)	(14.29)	(7.00)
Above middle	2	5	2	1	10
	(20.00)	(50.00)	(20.00)	(10.00)	5.00)

E. Caste status of respondents					
Lower	5 (9.26)	12 (22.22)	20 (37.04)	17 (31.48)	54 (27.00)
Middle	9 (9.28)	25 (25.77)	43 (44.33)	20 (20.62)	97 (48.50)
Upper	11 (11.34)	10 (10.31)	19 (19.59)	9 (9.28)	49 (24.50)
F. Socio-economic status of respondents					
Low	2 (4.44)	10 (22.22)	20 (44.44)	13 (28.89)	45 (22.50)
Medium	5 (4.24)	34 (28.81)	47 (39.83)	30 (25.42)	118 (59.00)
High	18 (48.65)	10 (27.03)	6 (16.22)	3 (8.11)	37 (18.50)

Figures in parentheses show their percentages to total

related livestock production than marginal categories. It may be due to the reason that women's of small category help received from servants on one hand and on the other dairying had been adopted as subsidiary occupation in many cases, thereby transferring many of the activities of males whom performed it on commercial basis. It was also found that the time spent by rural women in various tasks of livestock production was affected by a number of factors i.e. age, education, type of family, size of holding, caste and socio-economic status of respondents in both areas and categories. Respondents belonging to middle age (21-35 years) and upper middle age (36-50 years) groups participated more than lower and upper age groups. Respondents belonging to nuclear families spending more time in livestock production in comparison to joint families. Majority of respondent of both types of family spending 1-2 hours time per day. Participation of women in livestock production decreases with the increase in level of education. It is noted that more educated more spent less time in livestock production, due to reason of that they offer more time in other domestic activities. As regards caste status, respondents of middle castes participate more in comparison lower and upper caste. Respondents belonging to middle socio-economic status were participating more in activities related to livestock production than lower and upper socio-economic status. Amount of time devoted by women in livestock production system decreases with the rising level of socio-econoic status of respondent.

Policy Implications

It is suggested that suitable strategies should be developed at national, states as well as in the study area for the enhancing income, employment, standard of living and prosperity of rural women. For these purpose suitable varieties of short duration fodder crops and crossbred of different animals should be developed for different regions, which are suitable in particulars locality and conditions. It is also suggested that the special training programmes should be organised by the Government, Universities, Krishi Vigyan Kendra, NGOs and others institutions for the rural women to sustain livestock production in the country as well as state and regional level. These training programmes should be related to care & maintenance of livestock, better feeding stuff, animal healths, milking methods, preparing hay & silage, storage of dry & green fodder, storage of concentrates, and balance & maintenance diets of different categories of animals. All these efforts may be very helpful for rural women as well as their families in increasing income, employment, standard of living and prosperity of rural life.